How to Start, Run & Grow a Successful Restaurant Business

A Lean Startup Guide

By

Tim Hoffman

HERE IS WHAT'S INSIDE

I WANT TO OPEN A RESTAURANT

If you're good at what you do the restaurant business will give you a good living in a few years. Big profits don't come very fast let alone right away.

Do you dream about being your own boss? Do you enjoy food, waiting on people and have wanted to own a small business as long as you can remember? You feel passionate about turning nothing into something.

You have a lot of patience, good people skills, and don't mind working more hours than a full-time job. You can crunch numbers, clean, do accounting, empty the trash, wash dishes, deal with sales people and customers.

You're okay with being a jack of all trades. You are not swayed or scared, you are committed. You might even be a Chef wanting to strike out and show off your talent in your own restaurant.

Opening a restaurant isn't the objective, building a profitable restaurant that you have been dreaming about is the objective. Being prepared means that you will do a lot of planning. Financial plans, operational plans, marketing plans and the big one, business plans.

Maybe you're thinking, "Should I? I don't know where to begin". How about defining specifically what kind of restaurant you want to open, and why.

You know it's going to be a lot of work, but what fun! All your friends and family will come around to visit, it will be known as the top-in-its class style and food. It will be a nice little place in a cool neighborhood where lots of people will come in at least every week.

Doesn't that sound just so perfect, romantic and a fun place to go and work every day? Well, forget about that overnight dream for a few years. In fact, about 80% of new restaurants fail in three to five years. These failures include independent restaurants and some chains.

Unless Gordon Ramsey is coming by anytime soon, you'll have more headaches, heartaches, and gobs of numbers to deal with, more research and planning to do than you've ever had in your life! And, that's hardly the beginning.

Owning a restaurant means long hours, fast paced long weeks, there will be a lot of customer contact and you will be on your feet all day. Unless you are back in your office counting receipts, time cards, orders, equipment and pulling out your hair.

The important thing that you have going for you is that everybody eats. The next thing is that people don't want just to eat they also want to be entertained. They may want to go on a date, meet with clients, build social relationships, relax or just save time.

Another important thing going for you is that there are about 20,000 new restaurants opening a year, but, not all the innovative ideas have been taken. If there is an idea like yours, or the same, you just outperform them.

If you compete at the top, above all others with passion, commitment, great products and services you always have a chance.

"...opening a restaurant is a horrible, horrible, great idea..."

Food and Drink Magazine

You can even bring old products and services to your restaurant if you put your own unique spin on it, and deliver the product in a new way. You may carve out a niche for yourself. This is a good thing in the competitive restaurant industry.

Another important thing in your favor is that this is one of the most exciting times ever to open your own restaurant. There are zillions of new, and thrilling things happening in the food industry. Get ideas from the fresh and exhilarating crazes that true entrepreneurs are bringing to the forefront.

WHY VS WHAT

All restaurants have a brand. If you want your restaurant to thrive, you will have to make a fundamental commitment to foster and control your brand. Without your commitment, a plan or idea takes on a life of its own and loses focus.

Before we get into the nitty-gritty of all the work, which will lead to the joy of your passion, let's go over a basic psychological principle. You must know the difference between WHY and WHAT.

WHY and WHAT can be adapted to your whole life. In this case, it's applied to the restaurant you want to open. People don't buy WHAT you do, they buy the WHY.

To be successful and put your plan into action you must precisely define WHY you want to open a restaurant. Compared to WHAT you will do. Which is basically owning a restaurant, driving to it every day, working long hours, working your fingers down to nubs, and going back home. You sleep a few hours then start over.

You must be honest with yourself and commit to WHY you are taking on this life work. When WHY is fuzzy, the world is fuzzy. If you don't have a clear and concise idea of why you want to run your dream restaurant, you're starting a new restaurant already destined to fail.

Arm yourself with a mission statement, business plan stated goals and timelines. Then you have a direction. You can concentrate on success because you know where you are going.
Research is your friend, business planning is your friend, and, of course, money. But, without these things, you won't be able to concentrate on your dream. If you don't define the WHY, whatever plans you may will get confused and lost.

At that point, no one around you understands exactly what you want them to do. Everyone is confused, you're running in circles, and things keep going wrong. Growth gets difficult, at best, and failure and bankruptcy at worst.

Let's test it. Here's a conversation between two people at a cocktail party.

What do you do?
I own a restaurant.

What's the name of it?
Goose Chase.

Wow, cool name. What kind of food do you serve?
We have a family menu, everything from burgers to prime rib. You can get things to go, and sometimes we have a buffet.

That sounds like something for everybody.
Yeah, well.

What made you want to get into the restaurant business?

Money. I always thought about it and thought I could make a lot of money. You know, how hard can it be? And I'm my own boss.

How's it going? Is it as easy as you thought, are you having fun at it?

Not really. I work 60-80 hours a week. That's the time I'm not so sure about this whole restaurant no-fun idea, but I'll see how far I can go. Before it kills me

Eww, that doesn't sound good. Aren't you getting lots of new customers?

I don't think so. Right now, I basically just keep the place running. I'm kind of stuck in the background and can't keep an eye on everything.

Then, why do you keep doing it?

Money.

It just turns into a never-ending circle, doesn't it? Our friend doesn't give a WHY he goes through this.

Money? A given. But why suffer so much every single day? There is no passion expressed, and it's hard to see how this owner keeps going.

Spoil alert! Customers are not coming to your restaurant because you get in your car every day, drive to work, and stay there 60-80 hours a week, have no life, no friends, no vacations. That's WHAT you do.

Your customers are buying you. Your passion, your love of cooking (if true), your pride in presenting just the perfect little place, or providing lightning fast service.
You are providing the experience your customers will come back for. Offering creative thinking and quality food. Your love of serving good food, seeing people happy and making friends. That's a WHY.

If you're thinking about opening a restaurant, you probably eat out a lot. Why do you visit certain restaurants and keep going back? Why do you skip over others?

Add your own experiences to this list of why people keep going back to a favorite:

- Great food
- Location
- Comfort
- Ambience
- Cleanliness
- Fun place to meet friends
- Casual with lots of TVs
- Satisfying experience
- Great staff

What else? People want to feel like they belong and are appreciated. The wait staff is helpful to them. They are efficient, and the chef cooks food perfectly and/or fast.

Everything is clean and polished. The bartender is quick. Maybe there's a valet. The restrooms are clean, appropriate.

It took you 60-80 hours that week to provide that experience for your guests. Does that matter to your customers? No. Will they be back? Yes.

Test out your WHY on any kind of restaurant you want to put your heart and soul into.

For instance, people don't drive through McDonald's because McDonald's makes a ton of money all over the world, their staff is underpaid (not really, in some stores they make $16/hour) or that the manager just worked 80 hours that week. Does anyone care when they are just hungry and in a hurry?

Ask a Mom or Dad with an SUV full of kids what they are doing.
We're going to McDonald's.

Why?
Because we're hungry and in a hurry.

Why McDonald's?

Because they're fast, cheap and close by, we know what we are getting, and it's always the same.

That family just described the mission of McDonald's. You must figure out if you want to implement that plan. Would you put your heart and soul into making your McDonalds special?

According to Bloomberg, 75% of McDonalds' sales come from the drive-through window.

There's a story about one owner who knew there was something going on with his drive-through window. He couldn't quite put his finger on it. People were pulling into the parking lot, but the window wasn't living up to its potential.

He did his own little study. For a couple of days, including a weekend, he went outside, sat in his car and observed drive-through traffic at several rush hours on multiple days.

He found that during rush hours on designated days, the magic number was thirteen. When thirteen cars were in the drive-through line, approaching cars would turn around and leave.

Pretty soon after that, there were two extra employees outside at the drive-through line with electronic tablets taking orders.

At a reasonable pace, these employees would go up and down the line of waiting cars greeting the drivers. They would apologize for the wait and say they wanted to get the order straight to the kitchen for them to shorten their wait time.

They would greet the driver with something along the lines of, "...so we can help you get on your way," and "Thanks, and have a wonderful day."

The kitchen received the orders faster because there was no lag time. They didn't have to wait for the next driver to get to the speaker. Pretty soon cars were no longer turning around, and more than thirteen cars were served.

Why would this owner go to that much trouble? He owned the restaurant, he was the boss, made money, and corporate was happy. After all, McDonald's gets a lot of business just by being there, and people are always turning around anyway.

Did the customers know the effort and cost the owner put into this drive-through window project? Training for the employees, the tablets they used for taking orders? Most customers didn't care, think or worry about the time and expense it took. But they drove away feeling special.

It's true, the owner will make more money. But WHY? Because our friend didn't just own a restaurant. He wanted to be the one providing the best fast food experience for every customer.

The WHY should be your passion.

Don't try food service if you:

- Don't get the WHY you are in the business
- Have no passion for it
- Are only looking for glamour and fame
- Don't know the concept of commitment
- You can't write a business plan or read a financial statement
- You don't have any business experience, including management
- Don't want to work long hours
- Can't develop plans and goals
- Only cut up a few carrots in the kitchen now and then
- Can't delegate because nobody does it better than you
- Can't hold your temper
- Can't take criticism
- Don't know how to hire the right people
- Don't know how to treat people

Add your thoughts. This list can go on and on. You can see why restaurants fail but conversely you can see how yours can succeed.

Are you good with all of this? Well, maybe you're almost
ready to open your own restaurant!

DEVELOP A CONCEPT THAT WILL FLY

Your overall concept design is a critical decision. One of the biggest decisions about it is what kind of manager do you want to be?

Once you have an idea, it's clever to hire a restaurant concept design company, commercial designer, or architect. Whatever help you need, get it unless you are an expert. Even in that case you need a sounding board.

Professionals make all the parts fit. For instance, customers move all around a restaurant. They exit, enter, visit restrooms and use walkways. Employees exit and enter the kitchen, use the employee break room, etc. It takes an expert to map this out.

THE INDUSTRY TYPES OF RESTAURANTS

Research, research, research. Who is your target market? What will your menu, the heart of your restaurant, consist of? What price range are you thinking about? The name of your restaurant. What kind of service will you offer? Dine in, carry out, delivery?

Let's do a little run down on the styles or types of restaurants there are. First, here are some short and quick definitions, just to kick around some ideas for a concept. Definitions of the style and types of restaurants get blurred at times.

Sometimes what you think is Fast Casual sounds the same as Casual Dining. Then you may wonder, does Fast Food include Diners or are they Fast Casual? You'll have a better feel for this after you move through some of the definitions and characteristics of each type.

Set your mind on some cornerstones for your concept.
- Do not try to be everything to everyone!
- Make your concept clear to your customer.

- What is the specific kind of food you want to serve.
- Will you offer alcohol, and what are you thinking as far as a price range?
- Mostly, who is your audience?

Fast Food (QSR)

Fast Food focuses on speedy service. The range of this restaurant goes from small-scale street vendors to the gazillion dollar corporations like McDonalds and Wendy's.

Fast Casual

Fast Casual is the fastest growing here-to-stay trend in the industry. These are typically franchise and chain restaurants, like Panera Bread, Five Guys and Chipotle Mexican Grille.

More food is prepared at these locations than fast food locations, and there is no table service. Disposable plates, utensils, etc. are used. Prices and quality are higher than fast food, but lower than casual dining.

CASUAL DINING

The Casual Dining level restaurant has modestly priced food and a casual atmosphere. Like TGI Fridays for example and Olive Garden. If the restaurant is not buffet style, casuals provide table service, a large beer and wine selections and fun food.

FAMILY STYLE

The diners at the table agree on what to order, food is brought to the table in platters the diners pass around to each other. Family-friendly diners and casual restaurants fit into this category.

FINE DINING

These are full-service restaurants, with dedicated meal courses, high-end décor, and dress codes. Tablecloths and napkins, upscale food, upscale prices.

VARIATIONS

These are basically subsets.

- Barbeque
- Brasserie/bistro/café
- Buffet
- Catering
- Coffeehouse
- Destination
- Ethnic
- Family Style
- Table Top Cooking

- Pub
- Pop-Up
- Teppanyaki-style
- Food Truck

You want to be a unique owner. How will your concept, your restaurant, stand out from the competition? That is, the competition directly around you and the competition throughout your community.

Letting your creativity run free is one of the best parts of developing a concept. Your personality and uniqueness should be exactly what appeals to customers and draws them in and back again.

What kind of food will you serve? If a neighborhood has three breakfast and lunch places, it doesn't need another one. If there are two sandwich shops and a Subway, the area probably doesn't need another. If your target is 19-35-year-old females, a buffet won't work.

Think about this scenario. On a major, very busy street (four lanes each way including turn lanes) in a residential neighborhood, located on the east side of a large city, a popular shopping center sits. Population just for that part of the county, about 700,000. And customers come from all over.

A line of restaurants one after another, facing the street include Smokie's Barbeque, LongHorn Steaks, Macaroni Grill, Red Lobster and Friday's (TGIF). Can you figure that out?

Given these are chain restaurants and franchises there must be a reason they are all bunched up together. After all, they have big marketing machines paying out big dollars to identify profitable locations. Big, expensive stores in brick-and-mortar.

Who do you think is not moving into that lineup?

The reasons are location and target market. A small little street runs behind the restaurants to get into each parking lot for the restaurant of your choice.

Directly behind the restaurants and their parking entrances is the shopping center, anchored by a Super Target.

Across the big eight-lane street, is Home Depot, and in the opposite direction is Lowe's. Major pharmacies and other miscellaneous crowd pleasers run up and down the main drag.

The shopping center is at the exit and entrance ramps of the major toll road leading straight to downtown. Four miles or so from the location is a major university.

For miles around people and families of all ages and types see these restaurants, DIY stores and the shopping center every single day of their life. Typically, twice a day. Soccer moms, countless times.

These restaurants have the location down. They have the audience down. Their target market varies from singles, young adults, families, couples eating out before going to a movie, which happens to be at the back of that shopping center.

The types of food provided cater to those target markets. TGIF is a fast casual for younger groups, Red Lobster, a casual and usually appealing to older groups and families.

The barbeque place doesn't have competition for several miles and is unique in that neighborhood.

Macaroni Grill is Italian, appeals to almost everyone. Good family food, good date night place, and a large gathering restaurant.

These places just struck gold, but there's a story here.

In addition to a Super Target, the shopping center has over one hundred non-food retail outlets. Two pet stores, for instance, Best Buy, LA Fitness, middle to upper-end clothing and accessory stores.

Food outlets include Panera, Crispers Salad, two popular burger places, an ice-cream place, a Gelato window with lines around the block.

Starbucks, Toojays Deli with table service, a cookie place, Subway, a bagel place, Edibles and it goes on. There's a short strip of restaurants at a back entrance serving ethnic and other fast food. Small independent restaurants which are always busy. Except for the Chinese restaurant.

There never seems to be anyone inside. They have a few tables. Occasionally there are one or two people inside. Where is everybody? How can they stay open?

They stay open because all the staff is in the back busy preparing deliveries for the surrounding big residential area that continues to grow.

Oh yes, there's a great pizza storefront preparing delivery but also offering takeout. Not to be left out, McDonald's is just a hop, skip and a jump away.

Amigo's Mexican closed its doors in this shopping center after about five years. And, no other Mexican restaurant is close by. The famous Wahlburgers moved into Amigos' prime spot. They are open daily for lunch and dinner.

All of Wahlburgers' locations offer full-service dining, counter service, take out and a full-service bar. Sounds like a mini-Hard Rock.

You know what's not there? A small independent deli. Just, for example, one that has a front window, no tables, maybe one or two on the patio shared with the other restaurants in the row.

A display case and a couple of guys slicing cooked meats, maybe baking their own bread. People could stop on their way home from work and pick-up something hearty and unique.

Who is the competition? Subway? Toojays Deli? Subway is a fast food franchise. Toojay's is fast casual style. Jimmy John's delivers in the surrounding area.

How would you evaluate an opportunity like that? Would you do it?

Research mandatory. But, our unique Joe's Belly Deli could have warm roast beef subs with a special cheese and/or horseradish sauce and mushrooms. Italian subs or pastrami and cheese could be on the menu. Some kind of turkey and fixings. Maybe turkey and brie. And a big old-fashioned barrel of dill pickles.

Shoppers could pick-up lunch or dinner. Workers from surrounding businesses and all those college students are potential customers. Singles who don't have the time or don't want to go to a restaurant alone. A to-go place for picnic food.

If that deli was down the street a half mile or so from all the action would it be as successful?

Probably not, especially without a drive-through window. But then, all the charm and uniqueness would be lost.

You don't want to be in the middle of your competitors, but you want your very own uniqueness convenient to your target market in a profitable location.

Don't be a "Me too!"

You may have a general idea or already know how to get your dream project started. But again, and as you see over and over, a critical factor is the location. Hand and hand with location is the demographics of your location.

Is the area white or blue collar? Men, women, families? Professional workers, college students. What appeals to families with children isn't going to appeal to a place where single white-collar workers get together after work for drinks and dinner.

By identifying your target market, you further define your concept. Say you want to open an Indian restaurant. What location would be good for your city or community? How about seating capacity, parking, hours of operation, prices, menu, and décor?
There probably won't be a lot of children visiting so you could be open late. Maybe your décor would be an intimate, mysterious group of draped off areas. Or, with legitimate artifacts and décor from India. The wait staff respectfully dressed in theme.

Maybe it's located on a popular shopping street with a mix of one or two other restaurants and a few small boutique shops. Stores that are closed all night, where window shopping makes an after-dinner stroll more enjoyable. The type of street the British call a High Street.

Does this style of restaurant fit where you have chosen your location? Or, would you be better off opening an Indian to-go place in your location? Doesn't that sound like a pretty good service for an Indian Restaurant?

The location you love may not fit the theme or your concept. It may be too costly to build out or retrofit. So, you stay flexible. Finding the right location could take some time.

Along with location, you need to identify and know your potential customers. Start with some first-hand research. Visit the restaurants in and around your chosen location. Visit restaurants in your city with the same concept, similar menus, and pricing.

Who's coming and going? Do the kind of people going to change on the weekend? Are they different on weekdays? What kind of cars do they drive? How are they dressed?

Do they come in two's or four's? Families, a bunch of singles, are they reserved, laughing and enjoying the experience, or rowdy? How long do they stay? How many people are getting to-go orders?

Macaroni Grill has a call ahead and pick up service. A waitperson delivers your food to your car as soon as you pull up into their special parking spaces. Outback Restaurants have the same service. Observe them as well.

Go sit in a food court. Just observe people and what's going on around you. What kind of mall or shopping center is it. Just start somewhere.

Talk to any and all restaurant owners you can. Listen to people who even think your idea is stinky.

There's another group you should watch. Your concept will be impacted if you are close, or in the middle of tourist areas and attractions.

You need demographics on people visiting those

areas to round out
your concept; fortify
your business plan.

Do your own
research by
observation and
checking things
out. Take
advantage of
Hotel and Tourist
Association
information. Talk
to building
planners,
research city
plans.

Is a big
convention
center going in
close by?
Research what

the tourist
attractions have
planned.

Which way is the
community and
city growth
going? Toward
the city, away
from it, or are
they smack dab
in the middle of a
city?

Some research ideas to pinpoint income, median age
and household size around your location include the
US Census Bureau. Also, the Chamber of Commerce.
Some cities have other small business associations,
and you can always tap into the Small Business
Association.

If you have the budget, hire a small research
company or group who will implement a focus group

for you. The people in the focus group are consumers who will give you information, feelings, and opinions. People will talk more without you there. Don't be in the room.

"Well, I won't say anything, so they won't know who I am," you think. Don't kid yourself. The focus group attendees will pick up on that very quickly. It makes them think that something fishy is going on.

Often the facility scheduled by the marketing research company has a two-way mirror with sound piped into the observers' room on the other side of the mirror. Observe from there. You want to see body language if possible.

Focus groups are valuable. People are more responsive when asked questions directly. People are also most likely to share in a group than in a one-on-one situation.

If you cannot observe, the experts are good at reading body language and interpreting other movements. They will record and report back to you.

The goal is to get input from people of diverse perspectives and backgrounds.

Another focus of research is food trends. Your restaurant cannot be based on fads. The food trends to research are things like gluten-free, no GMO, organic, vegetarian options.

Are other restaurants with your theme or the competition around your location gearing up to serve breakfast? Do they deliver? Will you? Why or why not? You could, just to be different.

The Food Network and gourmet magazines like Gourmet and Bon Appetite are valuable resources. It is their job to report on and cover design and food trends, what's going on in the industry.

Watch celebrity Chefs!

Your concept should be something fun that you will love doing every single day of your life, never regret the decision, baby it, grow it, and make money at it.

Another major decision, something for your cornerstone, is what kind of owner do you want to be? For instance, a hard-number crunching, business-minded person might enjoy the franchise route.

Maybe you're a chef or hands-on cook wanting to showcase your skills and creativity in fine dining or in a very cool upscale casual. Or, maybe you are a charming people- person leading your guests into a superbly perfect dining room.

One thing you don't want to get stuck in is a fad. For instance, yogurt was a fad, and now those shops are gone. Tacos, even from a food truck, are established fare. They are evolving into fish tacos and other flavors.

You might just want to bring your ethnic food to the city or to your own community. There are many Little Vietnam, Little Havana, China Towns in major cities. These areas support independents. Have you ever seen a franchise in one of those areas?

Stay true to yourself and your concept. Do not stop until you have the perfect idea that reflects you, implement market research, and be precise in your theme. You won't get the funding you need if you are just blowing in the wind.

At the beginning of the Chapter, you read some short definitions of restaurant types. The 'type' is determined by the food industry. And, once again categories can get confusing. For instance, Wikipedia has a list of exactly one-hundred types of restaurants.

The food industry sets classifications based on preparation methods, menu style and, of course, pricing. The major types of restaurants include Fast Food, Fast Casual, Casual, Family Style, and Fine Dining. Followed by Buffets and variations of restaurant themes.

Here is a good example of the evolving food industry, and maybe a promising idea for you to consider. Shifting in the breeze is the talk of Fine-Casual and Fast-Fine Dining. You may have already seen it, but it hasn't hit you yet.

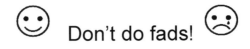 Don't do fads!

FAST FOOD OR QUICK SERVICE RESTAURANT (QSR)

FRANCHISE

A franchise is not the same as a chain of restaurants. McDonald's, Taco Bell, Wendy's are franchises. Chain restaurants, Starbucks and Panda Express, for instance, are owned by a single parent company and do not sell franchises. Some chains will consider new partners.

Franchises are supposedly 'turn-key" operations. That's why they're so expensive. You're buying the ready-made kitchen and dining room layouts and equipment, expensive marketing campaigns and name recognition.

You will need a franchise attorney. You need expert guidance, advice, and assistance. Do not use a broker. S(He) works for the franchisor and gets paid a commission. You need impartial experts.

In fact, you need your own impartial expert. This is the time to invest some money. Get a franchise attorney who is current on franchise legalese. Your attorney must be more than just familiar with franchise contracts. Get references.

Keep control of your situation. Once you have chosen a franchise, keep looking. Compare opportunities between franchises. And, compare opportunities between franchises and your own independent restaurant.

.

Franchise research and due diligence seriously lowers your financial risks. While you chew on that, let's look at the enviable McDonalds, as a high-end entry but universal model.
To be considered for a Mc/Donald franchise, you must have $500,000-$900,000 in liquid assets. The final number is based on the price of your franchise. The price of your franchise is based on size and location of your store.

Your liquid assets can include cash on hand, bonds, securities, debentures, equity in a business or real estate. Equity in real estate cannot come from your home.

Next, the initial investment to buy a McDonald's franchise is between $1.2 million and $2.2 million. This investment number depends on the size of the store, location, kitchen equipment needed, décor, landscaping, and signage plus your training.

While your franchise investment covers the above, McDonald's owns the actual building. You are paying for the build out.

Add an additional $45,000 as a franchise fee. Mostly, the franchise fee is a license to run a business under the McDonalds brand.

In return, you keep all net profits. Let's see how that works out.

Monthly, you pay a service or royalty fee of 4% of your gross sales to McDonalds Corporation. And, since McDonald's owns the McDonalds building, they are your landlord. Monthly rent is also based on a percentage of your gross sales.

The average per store sales is $2.5 million annually. Not profit, sales.

There are other available franchises that are a fraction of the cost compared to McDonald's. For instance, Papa John's Pizza, Jimmy John's, Pizza Hut, Chick-fil-A.

They work with the same basic model as McDonald's, but have a lower up-front investment cost, maybe a different build-out program. That's good news but beware. Some franchisors require you to open multiple new locations, typically within three years.

Here's a look at a one-location Subway franchise from WikiAnswers. Examples like this are just that and do not include your initial up-front costs.

Based on a Subway with $1000 (365k yearly) average sales per day:

Gross sales per year
$365,000

40% of 365k for royalties and food
146,000

4000 average rent for 12 months
48,000

Electricity, insurance average
for 12 months (1400*12)
16,800

Garbage, telephone, accounting
and misc. for 12 months (500*12)
6,000

Employee's salary for
12 months (5000*12)
60,000

Sale Tax (NY) 8.5% on gross sales
29,200

(306,000)

Net profit before tax
$ 59,000

Take a second look. At eighty hours a week, you are working 4,160 hours annually. Your gross income is $59,000. Divide that by 4,160 and you are making $14.00 an hour.

You can juggle the numbers, work fewer hours and work out different rent, etc. But, in the end, if you're looking at a single franchise location with no plan to expand you might want to buy stock instead.

Seasoned franchisees say that profits are in the number of locations you own. Meaning, the key to profitability is scale. The total profits from each location nets bigger profits for you by using economies of scale.

Typically, franchising gets easier after the third location. At that point, you can hire a manager. By your fifth, you can hire a regional manager. Because of economies of scale, you can shift employees around as needed.

Investigate franchises that continually rate high in the top ten. For food. Explore new options. Other ideas about franchises may fit into your concept, or hatch a new idea. The top 'usual ones' are not always the top best for you.

A couple of years ago, *Consumer Reports* surveyed 32,000 readers eating 96,000 meals. Those meals were eaten at chains and franchises. The participants graded each on a score out of 100. Here are a few, no scores:

Papa Murphy's

Surprise. According to the survey, Papa Murphy's ranks as the best fast food pizza. It's quirky and has a cost-effective hitch. They are a take-and-bake franchise pizzeria, selling a large pizza for $8.00. Customers come in, buy their pizza, go home and bake it. This significantly reduces operational costs for the restaurant owner. The franchise is notable for quality food, staff politeness, and fast service. Minimal franchise set-up.

Chick-fil-A

Chick-fil-A is the hottest big chain in the country, says Jonathan Maze, On the Margin blog. Open six days a week, closed at night and still growing at an astounding rate. Over the last five years, Chick-fil-A sales increased almost 73%. This is a jump from $4.6 billion to $7.9 billion in system-wide sales.

Specializing in chicken sandwiches, Chick-fil-A has been named the best fast food in America by Consumer Reports.

For an initial fee of $10,000 selected franchises obtain the right to operate one of their franchises. Additional information is on their website with a very interesting franchise structure.

Jason's Deli

Operates with a deli-style menu. Sandwiches, soups, and salads. The company has removed all trans fats, MSG and high fructose corn syrup from its entire menu. It rated in the top ten for the quality of food, cleanliness of dining area and polite staff.

Started by two partners, 60% of the locations are company owned. Franchises carry an initial franchise fee of $17,500 granting the license for you to do business under their name, plus an initial investment of $680,000-$905,000.

Take a minute and check out their website. It is beautiful. It may give you some ideas for yours. At http://www.chainstoreguide.com there are reports and directories to help you find information on franchises. The information will include the status of a company and financial information. This is valuable information where you can compare the franchises against each other.

An extensive list of franchises can be found at www.entrepreneur.com. There are hundreds of business magazines onsite with valuable information, including magazines specific to franchising and restaurants.

If franchising is your dream, the best information to start with is on the company's franchise website. Not all franchises have to cost the moon. There are so many new, fresh franchise opportunities you may find one that suits your palette.

Franchise.city.com helps buyers find franchises in their price range. There are other sites as well, but do your research before signing anything.

THE DELI AND SANDWICH SHOP

Delis and sandwich shops sometimes get thrown into fast food and other times into fast casual. These are not all franchises, but independent food service establishments as well.

As the second fast-food concept, sometimes a deli or sandwich shop will have one side as a deli/sandwich area, and the other side with tables.
(Think of it as same food, different distribution system)

Delis and sandwich shops work great in busy downtown areas. The target audience is working professionals and other workers in all the surrounding businesses. The big sales peak is between 11 a.m. and 2 p.m.

The business model is based on convenience and quality food at a reasonable price. These two types of restaurants are housed in informal spaces and provide delivery, take out, and take home.

Location is critical. You need a storefront and display case in a busy area. When working your numbers keep in mind that a higher rent location may produce additional foot traffic. You cannot be stuck in a location that is out of sight.

Sandwich shops and delis rely on repeat business. Study your estimated revenue and expenses for a specific location. Then decide if the higher rent of that location justifies a lower profit margin. Remember that any decision is going to affect your ROI.

Quality food is critical in delis and sandwich shops, but pricing is not as sensitive. The industry reports that people do not trust low-priced deli or designer sandwiches. If the price is reasonable patrons will pay for extra quality food.

Typically, delis have a theme such as Jewish or German, much like the ones opened by our early immigrants. Sandwich shops are open to your own interpretation and market demand. Either way, you need a new emphasis and menu concept beyond the usual salads and sandwiches.

You could elevate your menu to emphasize local foods and artisan bread. Highlight products that enforce your theme, maybe from Germany or Italy. To stay competitive, add unique options, for instance, desserts matching your theme.

Fast casuals are quickly implementing unique twists on breakfast offerings. One example is that Caribou Coffee has introduced a quick serve quiche.

You can do the same thing at your deli and or sandwich shop. Adding convenient breakfast items would boost sales and awareness. You may get additional walk-in business by opening a little earlier offering quick breakfast items. Is it possible to offer breakfast like that cost-effectively? Well, what if your deli ordered pre-made items from a local bakery? Maybe if you name the bakery somewhere in your shop, they will give you a discount.

If it were a famous bakery in your community, not too close to your location, your items add even more swank. If the bakery isn't open before you, more the better. Your discount is simply a marketing expense for the bakery, and more profit for you.

Along the same lines as the above pre-made bakery items and bread, delis/fast casuals can offer popular labeled goods along with their descriptions. Using name brand meat, for instance, or descriptions of where your products are from express a pledge of quality to your customers.

This tactic builds on a deli/fast casual's market positioning by offering better-quality and limited-service fare. The stakes have been raised. It's imperative that you are aware of these trends. How food and the food service industry is evolving. And how you can outsmart and profit from them.

COURTESY OF QSR MAGAZINE

For 25-unit Modern Market, adding breakfast was a no-brainer. "We had staff coming in at 6 a.m. to prep for lunch, so we just redirected one or two people to serve people coming in," says chef Nate Weir, adding that the breakfast crowd tends to include college students, suburban moms, and workers heading to the office.

When developing the menu, Weir also redirected many of the ingredients already on hand to create items such as the veggie-loaded Scrambles, with charred broccoli, caramelized onions, aged white cheddar cheese, and pastured eggs. The only equipment change was the addition of a toaster and some dedicated coolers for breakfast.

"At the same time, you must balance operational complexity," Weir says. "We're not training short-order cooks who can bang things out, so we start our eggs right away and then just add the other elements, so our customers can pop in and get an amazing egg dish or sandwich and be out the door in five minutes."

In addition to packaged goods, or instead of packaged goods, fast casuals use ingredients on hand. Could you offer a ham and cheese breakfast sandwich with ingredients you use every day and are conveniently on hand?

Maybe an extra employee could come in early with the rest of the set-up crew and just make special breakfast items. How about a veggie breakfast sized sandwich with Greek vanilla yogurt as a side?

Get away from the ubiquitous eggs-sausage-cheese on an English muffin. Croissants and biscuits could stay. That local bakery, how about fresh baking of biscuits? How about cheese, tomatoes, and sprouts on various breads?

The thing about an unusual variety is that you could cause a 'frenzy.' Offer a limited number of various sandwiches switching up items every few days. Pretty soon that walk-in traffic may compete for certain sandwiches on expected days.

Sandella's Flatbread Café

Headquartered in Connecticut, but no longer franchising. Sandella's offers the West Coast Panini breakfast sandwich. It features egg, tomatoes, baby spinach, cheddar Jack cheese, avocado and chipotle sauce.

This would be a huge undertaking for a deli. Although possible for a sandwich shop. This example is not a recommendation for a deli to take on this big of a process.

The point is to find a creative way to offer something as unusual but in an easy to carry out a miniature replica.

For a deli or sandwich shop élite offering, you could name specialty sandwiches after yourself and your employees. You still offer your regular fare on a daily basis. But, add your own twist. Have certain specialty sandwiches on different days, identified by employee names.

For instance, various sliders for breakfast using ingredients on hand. Maybe that turkey and brie are not what you want to offer daily. A combined Chicken and BLT. How about prepackaging these for lunchtime take away.

You could also consider a few items for breakfast or lunch to cater to surrounding offices that you deliver to office meetings. Orders could be called into you, with a cut-off time to order. That early arriving employee could work on those orders maybe even with your help!

FAST CASUAL

As mentioned above, Delis and Sandwich Shops are typed as a Fast Food and sometimes as

Fast Casual. Those blurred lines again. This Fast Casual section has ideas that can also be used for delis and sandwich shops.

It takes a lot of skill to offset high-quality food with fast and efficient service. The cornerstone of Fast Casual restaurants. The challenge is to keep it simple but unique.

As a step above fast food offering gourmet breads and fresh ingredients, fast casual restaurants can be a franchise or your independently owned restaurant. Some franchises are:

- Boston Market
- Five Guys
- Newk's Eatery
- Shake Shak
- Café Rio Mexican
- Schhlotzsky's
- Pollo Tropical
- Panda Express
- Baja Fresh Mex

- Elevation Burger
- Panera Bread
- Fazoli's
- Freshii
- Chopt
- Zaxby's

See if you might be interested based on this information from Euromonitor International:

- Industry estimates for prices at a fast-casual restaurant can be as much as 40% higher than a comparable fast food restaurant.

- The market for fast-casual food has grown by 550% since 1999.

- Last year, Americans spent $21 billion at fast casual restaurants.

- Consumers will continue to drive high volume sales, preferring to pay more for higher quality meals and restaurant hygiene.

- And, according to the NPD Market Research Group, fast-casual restaurants will grow by double-digits through 2022.

During the same growth period, Chipotle sales quadrupled, Panera more than tripled, and Shake Shack did so well it went public with only thirty-six outlets. Fast-casual is currently experiencing phenomenal growth not being seen in the QSRs.

The growing trend of fast casual was embodied by places like Chipotle, Fuddruckers's and Panera. Chipotle led the way with the business model, but, unfortunately for them, they are now in the last place. For everything.

The essential component for fast casual is the price point. Fast-casual meals run about $9 to $13 per ticket, versus $7 per ticket at a QSR. Fast casuals preferably earn less than 50% from sit-down meals or full service. Any more than that and it becomes a sit-down restaurant and costs go up, profits down.

Fast-casual mixes affordability with high-quality food. Unique features include made-to-order meals with customization options. Healthier ingredients that are fresh, organic and non-GMO.

Other elements of fast-casual dining include:

Disposable plastic products

Customization of meals

Higher quality ingredients

Higher quality food

Convenience

Visible kitchen

The following fast casuals represent a few of the country's top ten and a few out-of-this-world unique fast casuals. Look at these on-fire concepts from people thinking out of the box.

The Habit Burger Grill

Prepares fresh, made-to-order sandwiches and chargrilled burgers featuring USDA choice tri-tip steak. Sushi-grade albacore tuna and grilled chicken cooked over an open flame. There are more unique offers, but Habit Burger Grill has been named the "best tasting burger in America" by *Consumer Reports.*

Potbelly Sandwich Works

Started out of an antique shop, ended up a publicly traded company. Potbelly sells basic subs with a dozen sides for customization by the customer. Their target demographic is the lunch market. Soups, shakes, salads, live music and an old-wood décor are found at this unique eatery.

Marination Station

Offers Hawaiian-Korean bowls, burgers, and buns. A truck-to-restaurant fast casual mix. Several food trucks called Big Blue Park around town, and there are also a few brick-and-mortar locations in Seattle. Two tacos and a slider, $10.00. Started and owned by one couple, serving scratch-based street food.

Urban Plates

Offers twelve sides for patrons to customize their food. Entrees range from chimichurri grass-fed steak, turkey meatloaf with house barbeque sauce, and the newest addition habanero mango barbeque ribs. Urban Plates has hired the former Maître de of New York's celebrated Per Se restaurant, as their director of hospitality.

The industry shows that fast casual is the exciting, and fastest growing of all restaurant categories. It's creative and of the moment with great growth potential.

There's a huge choice among franchises and

to the moon

ideas and

themes for your

own

fast casual

restaurant.

Five Guys

Offers hand-made burgers and fresh-cut fries. Founded by celebrity Chef Danny Meyer, Five Guys started with one shop in Washington, DC. Now owned by the Murrell family, it is a national phenomenon with over 1,000 locations. No glitz, but the key to success for Five Guys is: Do one thing and do it well.

Innovating fast casual independents and chains are working to gain new revenue streams. They do so by staying competitive and offering breakfast items that are cost-effective, convenient and to go. Are they competing with the large franchises who have been in the breakfast arena for years?

Think about it. Big franchises do what corporate says, no choice, no creativity. Consistent product, the same everywhere and changes are like turning a battleship around. Breakfast is usually the most profitable meal at food outlets.

If you owned an independent fast casual restaurant or a chain, would you consider adding breakfast? If it was a new concept for you how would you react? Oh, you creative entrepreneurs! Roll up your creative sleeves and get to work.

Flexibility is an ace in the hole for the independent.

Approach adding any new product the same way as when you first opened your new restaurant. Who would be your target audience? Is there a market around your location? What would be the cost and would it be profitable enough?

Just saying would it be worth it? You will need a unique approach, a unique location, or both, and minimal or no new equipment.

As an independent how does your direct competition serve breakfast? Things to consider, do you have a drive through? Do you rely on a walk-in, walk-past business? Would economies of scale be advantageous? In what ways could you position yourself as a cut above the rest?

As discussed, the biggest things you have over the fast food outlets is pricing, flexibility, and control over what you serve. If you're a fast-casual, independent restaurant, you're the boss. And, across the breakfast menu, fast-casual concepts have room to innovate and differentiate.

Fast casuals are already elevating breakfast with limited use of quality buns, scrambles, and bowls, as well as healthier options. In addition to upping breakfast a notch or two, the fast casuals are developing deliberate strategies to produce new revenue with the addition of breakfast.

Using ingredients on hand like delis and sandwich shops, fast casuals can offer Veggie Scrambles with caramelized onions, charred broccoli, and cheese. This not only represents economies of scale but also ways to set yourself apart from the competition. You need creativity added to your concept to thrive.

These concepts take advantage of the economies of scale discussed. With these strategies, the fast-casual can cross-utilize on-hand ingredients and make small staff rearrangements. This is a progressive concept that adds an alternative revenue source without adding a lot of costs.

You can't afford to get on the 'me too' business wagon. Keep in mind that research has shown the optimal price a consumer will pay for a fast-casual breakfast is $6.01. But, fast food consumers think $4.50 is good, and $4.82 is high.

In a Technomic poll last year, one-third of surveyed consumers said they ate breakfast sandwiches at least once a week and some more often. That means sandwiches might fit into your picture. Remember, from the beginning of this adventure you know you need to embrace flexibility.

Nipping at the profits of your fast-casual restaurant is the growing trend of Grocerants. A combination of grocery store and restaurant. Basically, a grocerant is a food item that is ready to eat or taken home and heated, or several items are taken home to make up a full meal. The big draw is convenience and price.

Spoonity reports that 40% of the US population prefers to buy their prepared food from grocery stores. Grocerants have especially attracted Millennials, the least likely generation to rely on grocery stores.

Traditionally, prepackaged meals are in the deli section of the grocery store or a convenience store's prepared food section. While they may not be a threat to brick-and-mortar QSRs, note their locations relative to yours.

Grocerants don't incur the cost of operating a restaurant and don't want to. But, easy pick-up prepared or packaged meals are cost effective for the consumer and the grocerant.

The average grocerant meal is around $5.00. A comparable QSR restaurant meal is around $7.00. Do you think you want to compete with the grocerant concept?

Would that be in direct conflict with your brand image? You decide based on your original idea. But, remember, your concept will be successful if you stay brand-strong and never try to be all things to all people.

CASUAL DINING

Examples of casual dining restaurants are Applebee's, Red Lobster, Cheesecake Factory, Carrabba's Italian Grill, TGIF, Red Robin, Dave and Buster's, Outback and Longhorn Steak Houses.

In some cases, you will see these restaurants categorized as Family Style. What they mean is that those restaurants are family friendly. Food is plated by the kitchen, and table service is provided.

The traditional Family Style is the concept of serving large platters of food to the table, and the diners pass them around and share. The same examples, as previously mentioned, are Korean and Chinese. However, Olive Garden has a successful campaign for family dining.

As it turns out, casual dining is everything between fast food and fine dining and averages about $15 per meal. Characteristics are:

- Table service
- Moderately priced menus
- Full bar independent of the dining room

Whatever concept or type of restaurant you open, the very basics of any successful restaurant are and will remain great food, great service, and great people.

FINE DINING

What images do you conjure up when you hear Fine Dining?

Fine dining has three foremost parts: atmosphere, menu, and service. Your customer service requires world-class attentiveness. This is the most expensive restaurant to own and operate.

Everything about fine dining is in a class of its own. Customers are demanding and expect the worthiness of your prices:

World class entrance with Maître de verifying reservation and seating of diners

Diners are escorted to their table

Hold the chair for women

Escort diners to the restrooms

Clean crumbs (crumbing) between courses

If a diner leaves the table, replace the linen

Of course, food is served directly on the plate at table

The highest of quality food

Food may require assembling or cooking at tableside

Crisp white table linens

Maybe waiters in tuxedos

Fine china, polished, sparkling fine glassware/crystal

Polished, fine flatware

The details involved must be well-trained staff, ability to answer questions about the menu, drinks, etc. without notes. They must be able to make recommendations off the menu if asked. This often requires the wait staff to go through a tasting in the kitchen before service begins.

No detail is ever too small to take care of by the fine dining restaurant staff. Questions, taxis, valet, phone, messages. Never should a diner ask for a clean glass, plate, napkin, flatware, etc.

Fine dining establishments are most frequently used for special occasions. Business executives host important clients. A big date night, scene of a proposal for marriage. Events that are very special to your patrons, and they expect, demand the finer points that are offered.

It used to be that fine dining was a French restaurant. Almost exclusively, but not necessarily nowadays. While maintaining the standards of fine dining, you can set your restaurant in any setting and feature a variety of fare.

Local, organic or ethnic food, seafood, steaks, for example. It's your restaurant. You can go the traditional route or a colorful hip and trendy atmosphere with of the moment furnishings.

No matter what the food is that you serve it must be different from what diners would find in other restaurants. Distinctive, attractive and exciting. Locally sourced food is a growing trend and prix fixe menu items that change frequently.

Menus should not be large but fit with the seasons and your chef's specialties. You must serve fine wines and beer. Not Bud Light or coffee flavored brandy. Beer should be micro-brewed and unusual. All of these including liquors must be top shelf and compliment every menu item.

That means champagne, wines specific to the various courses, dessert wines, after-dinner drinks, brandy, cognac and specialty coffees. Regular and decaf coffee, élite teas that the diner selects from a wooden presentation box. Possibly cigars.

Don't cheap out here. Your customer will know immediately. And, it will ruin the quality of your food, your reputation. It just isn't worth it. Even the water you serve should be bottled, possibly served tableside with a wine cooler.

Appropriate music should mirror your theme. Subtle lighting, on the romantic side. Do what you can to make your restaurant above and beyond what is expected, go the extra mile. The restaurant doesn't have to be huge. You can start small. In the end, wouldn't it be great if diners had to make reservations a week, or a month ahead to dine at your restaurant.

Here is an example of a fine dining Dinner Menu, courtesy of La Truffe Sauvage, Lake Charles, Louisiana

Summer 2017

Tue.-Sat. 6:00p-10:00p

Appetizers

Crispy Duck Leg Confit 19.5 ^{GF}
creamy risotto, red wine sauce

Pan Sauté Crab Cake 16.5
vegetable noodles, créole rémoulade

Natural Sea Scallop au Gratin 14.5
à la Rockefeller

Chef's Assortment of European Cheeses 15.5
Gruyère, Gorgonzola Dolce, Roquefort and goat cheese

with toasted baguette, butter & walnuts

Pan Seared Moulard Duck Foie Gras 24.5
on dried fruit brioche with Granny Smith apple terrine, blood orange reduction

Soups

Gratin of Onion with Thyme, Garlic Crostini & Gruyère
9.5

Maine Lobster Bisque en Croûte 12.5

Consommé du Canard 12.5

Granny Smith apple, beef & fresh herb ravioli, white truffle oil

Salads

Mediterranean 10.5

vine ripe tomato, English cucumber, Valbreso feta, Kalamata olives,

capers, avocado, red onion & oregano vinaigrette

Chèvre Chaud over Baby Spinach 10.5

sauté breadcrumb crusted goat cheese, with toasted baguette,

pine-nuts, dried figs & roasted shallot vinaigrette

Caesar in a Crisp Parmesan Cheese Basket 10.5

La Truffe Sauvage House 10.5

mixed baby greens, Belgian Endive, Granny Smith apple,

Roquefort cheese, walnut vinaigrette

Main Course

Pot au Feu de Poisson aux Fenouilles et Curry 32.

with tomato, cream, shrimp, scallop, mussels, littleneck clams & fresh fish

Pan Roasted Wild Gulf Red Snapper 34.

steamed potato, sundried tomato, artichoke, capers, asparagus tips, lemon butter sauce & jumbo lump crab

Tournedo Rossini 58.

on dried fruit brioche, Madeira wine sauce

Slow Braised Beef Short Rib 34.

14 oz. single bone short rib, Gorgonzola dauphinois potato,

asparagus, French green beans, carrot, natural jus

Jumbo Lump Crabmeat Mary Louise 34.

crabmeat tossed in a champagne cream sauce and served in a puff pastry shell with asparagus

Pan Seared Dover Sole 44.

saffron steamed potato, asparagus, haricot vert, lemon butter sauce

Filet of Prime Beef Tenderloin 44. **GF**

Gorgonzola dauphinois potato, tomato, broccoli rabe, sauce Bordelaise

Pan Sauté Almond Crusted Softshell Crab 32.

over crab & cheese grits, asparagus, meunière sauce

Assorted Organic Mushroom Risotto with White Truffle Oil 28.5 **GF**

King Oyster, White Beech, Brown Beech & Hen of the Woods

wilted baby spinach & shaved Parmigiana Reggiano

SIDES 8.

fresh spinach sauté in olive oil **GF**

shaved brussel sprouts with olive oil & lemon **GF**

gorgonzola dauphinois potato **GF**

steamed asparagus **GF**

French green beans almandine **GF**

ratatouille **GF**

We are happy to prepare whole plant food dishes with Chef's Creation

Soufflé of the Evening 10.5 ^{GF}

please allow 30 minutes

NO SEPARATE CHECKS - multiple parties sharing the payment are accepted

GF - GLUTEN FREE (Some other menu items can be modified to accommodate a gluten-free diet.)

† Consuming raw or undercooked meat, seafood or egg products can increase your risk of foodborne illness.

815 West Bayou Pines Drive

Lake Charles, LA 70601

(337) 439-8364

WHERE TO FIND A RESTAURANT TO BUY OR LEASE?

If you are new to restaurant business but have enough interest to dig deeper, then the next step for you is to try and find a few businesses for sale and evaluate them the best way possible and see if any of them fit your budget and needs.

Restaurant is truly a recession-proof business and still provides a comfortable living for a family. Not to mention the freedom it provides by having and owning your own business.

If you are serious about finding a suitable restaurant business to buy or lease, there are many ways to find a few that are for sale in your area.

You can try both Online and Offline ways.

5 OFFLINE WAYS TO FIND A BUSINESS FOR SALE

- Through Local business brokers (Some national and some local. Two of the major national brokerage companies are Sunbelt and Nationwide business brokers. Local or statewide)

- Through Local commercial real estate agents
- Through Local newspaper classified
- Through Local or national food franchise offerings
- Through Vendors (this works better if you are already in this line of business)

5 Online Ways to Find a Business for Sale

There are some very reputable websites you can go and check for sale listings; then there are also online auction houses that sell restaurants among other businesses.

1. First, check out bizbuysell.com. This site is similar to realtor.com for home real estate, but in this site, business brokers list their businesses that are for sale.

2. Try searching on NRC.com and Loopnet.com. Both of these are big players when it comes to the online business brokerage. You will find both "for sale stores" and "for Lease stores."

3. Craigslist ads. Yes, you can find them under "business for sale."

4. Do a search for auction houses that sell commercial properties

5. You can also just do a google search by typing "restaurant for sale in Los Angeles, Ca" Just mention your city and state and see what comes up.

But before you contact any of the sellers or brokers, you need to have your game plan set, so you don't sound like you are just browsing the market.

Business brokers are very different than typical home real estate agents. If a broker senses that you are not serious, they may not even disclose some of their prime listings to you. The reason is simple; they don't want to take a buyer who is not serious to a seller who is motivated to sell. This can take away from the broker's credibility in front of the seller. Also, sellers typically only want serious and qualified buyers that are ready to buy.

You will notice that, before a broker discloses any information about a business, they will want you to sign a document called an NDA (Non-Disclosure Agreement). This is required because you are being exposed to some confidential and sensitive financial information about a business. Once you sign the NDA, you are in a contract that says you are not to disclose the information you are about to receive with just anyone.

Also, another thing to keep in mind when visiting any of the potential stores for sale, that most times the business owners do not want the employees to know that they are selling the business. Sometimes there is a good reason for it. So first sit down and figure out what your budget is, what your game plan is, and how soon you want to get into a business. Once you know these three, you are halfway there.

Just remember when you contact a business broker, they may ask you a lot of questions to figure out what, exactly, you are looking for. They may ask about your budget; it is usually a good idea not to answer that with a dollar figure, instead tell them that it varies depending on what is out there. This way they will show you a wide range of businesses. Some may be over your budget, and some below, but this way you can see where the market stands. It gives you a baseline of the highs and the lows of your market.

Once you have a list of 3-4 businesses to look at that is when your real work starts. First, you need to visit all the locations, so you have a visual feel for them. Take plenty of notes; best is to take notes where you write down the good the bad on each side so later you can see what the good points are and what the bad points are of a business and if the bad ones outweigh the good ones.

You can also use a marketing tool I often use called a MA-CP grid, where you draw a square box with 4 mini squares that are equal to the square in that big box and, on the left of this box, I write MA, which stands for market attractiveness and on the bottom I write CP or competitive positioning. I try to place each of the restaurant in one of those squares based on their location, sales, nearest competitors, etc.

If a restaurant has very high market attractiveness, you should place it on the high side of the quadrant. Similarly, if a store has a very good competitive position in the market, it should be placed at the "high" side as well. Ideally you want to pick the store/business that ranks high on both market attractiveness and competitive positioning. This way you know you are looking at a winner.

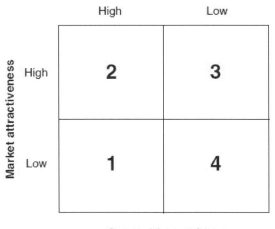

Competitive position

Once you narrow down to, let's say, 1-2 restaurants out the 5, time to tell your broker or seller that you are interested in finding out more about their business.

If you have come this far, then you are well on your way to be a business owner soon. But before you say yes, remember, once you narrow down to a handful restaurants, time to do a thorough due diligence on each of your findings.

Once you do good and thorough work, the right one will come out of that bunch, and you will know which business is the right one for you to make an offer on.

POP-UPS AS A TEST

For 2017, the new Best Restaurant in the World has just been announced. Eleven Madison Park (EMP), New York has been named the Best Restaurant in North America and the Best Restaurant in the World.

Immediately after receiving the coveted award, EMP closed its doors with a bang-up world-class party. The reason is the restaurant is being gutted and re-designed. Here's the kicker: In the meantime, the restaurant is going to East Hampton to open the EMP Summer House Pop-Up.

Upscale in every term for a pop-up, they have indoor and outdoor dining areas, a core idea of a seafood based menu, a tent out back for barbeques of lobster, burgers, and fish. And, of course, there are large format events on the beach.

You may not have had that in mind. But, if the World's Best Restaurant can do it, you can, too. Use your own concept, creativity, and purpose.

Pop-Ups are usually a short event. One or two days, over a three-day weekend, or opened for a fundraiser or community event. You can open one to test your concept and your food, get experience in setting up a mobile kitchen, figure out where to prep and serving details.

This is a chance to learn your abilities and create buzz about your new restaurant. On the other hand, you could run one for a couple weeks as a dry run for your restaurant and experience setting up a longer-term location.

Chefs, the young and/or experienced, may open a Pop-Up to build their reputation and/or try out new menu items. Existing restaurants could use a Pop-Up to test out new menus and food items. Others, such as new restaurant owners, caterers even food trucks can use a Pop-Up to lure investors.

Some restaurant owners, even a new person, trying out the food service field, use Pop Ups to offer gourmet food at a reasonable price and for the public to try out. See if it flies. Caterers can test out new concepts. It could just be a cocktail party.

If a location passes cooking and food safety a Pop-Up can be anywhere. They are usually opened in a former restaurant space. Another option is to rent a restaurant during their closing hours, as cheap as possible.

Retail space might be an option. You need your mobile kitchen, water, electricity, tables, chairs, and more. You'll need storage, prep and cooking space. These are all good opportunities to try if you really love the food service industry.

Another option is to rent a restaurant that only offers one or two services a day. For instance, a diner or small mom-and-pop restaurant that only sells breakfast and lunch. You could offer dinner and supper. Negotiate a percentage of your profits so the owners can cover their operating costs for keeping the building open.

Pop-Ups typically use the prix fixe style of menu. You may be limited on space, busy and stressed. Stick to anything that makes your event run smoothly. Go prix fixe instead of the hassle of a la carte.

People visit Pop Ups because they are fun and an adventure. It's an opportunity to try something creative, fresh and new and distinctive. Something that is different from the usual restaurant scene. Use a chalkboard, white board or inexpensive menus printed off your computer to announce and describe your food offerings.

There may be insurance issues, and temporary permits you will need to operate depending on the location. Keep it legit. There have been Pop Ups opened in airplane hangars, city rooftops, and one to test vegan ice cream.

It costs about $2,500 depending on your part of the country. The $2,500 should cover rent, insurance, and ingredients. No salary, you work for free. Paid staff could be available from various locations. Their day off, friends of friends, etc. You get the experience without going broke.

People follow Pop Ups, where they are, where the move to, nightly or daily specials and to make reservations. You can put up an inexpensive website and use small neighborhood independent shopper magazines.

Social media is the place to advertise. You can do some smaller things like posters and handouts, and word of mouth is good. But Facebook, Twitter, blogosphere, etc. are your best bet.

LEGAL STRUCTURE

How will you structure your new business? First, use an attorney throughout the process. Businesses can be structured as one of five categories.

1. Sole Proprietorship

This means that your restaurant will be run by one person. This is a typical option for small businesses. It may be a simple and inexpensive business structure, but it will increase your personal liability, and cost you major dollars in tax advantages.

2. Partnership

Here is where two or more people share talent, profits, and risk. While more complex than sole proprietorship there are some advantages but there are added liability and tax issues.

3. Corporation, or C-Corp

This is a legal entity that is separate from you(r) owners. A corporation can own property, assimilate debt and be sued. Set up of a C-Corp is expensive, but it provides better tax advantages and reductions in liabilities.

4. **Limited Liability Company, or an LLC**

   LLCs are growing more popular because they have several of the benefits of a partnership and corporations alike.

5. **Subchapter S-Corporation**

   This is a structure that incorporates you under state laws. You acquire the same tax benefits as a C-Corp. But in an S-Corp there are no corporate tax returns. Profits and losses are spread among the shareholders. This structure can be confusing since you can elect to be S-Corp at the federal level.

Before deciding your legal structure be clear about the following:

- Who are the owners?

- What liability protection do you need?
- How will earnings be distributed?
- What are your financing arrangements?
- What opening costs and requirements will you bear?
- How will your chosen legal structure affect your tax strategies?

FEDERAL AGENCIES

There will be a lot of legal paper and matters to deal with. Make sure your attorney is involved as you start up. Federal agencies you will deal with are the Department of Labor, Bureau of Alcohol, Tobacco and Firearms (BATF) and, of course, the IRS.

⚖ Department of Labor

Sometimes called the Labor Board. This branch of the government administers the U.S. Labor Standards Act. They make sure you comply with the federal minimum wage, overtime, hiring teenagers and managing the Equal Employment Opportunities Commission or EEOC. EEOC deals with acts of discrimination.

A second branch of the Department of Labor is OSHA, Occupational Safety and Health Administration. They inspect workplaces and assure that employees are trained in their health and safety rights.

Along these lines, the Department of Immigration and Naturalization Services, assures that all employees have documentation to work in the United States.

**The IRS**

You know the IRS will collect taxes from your business, you and your employees. You need an Employer Identification Number or EIN. This is your business' equivalent to your personal social security number. The IRS tracks your restaurant by this number to make sure you pay the required estimated federal income taxes on a quarterly basis, as well as FICA or Social Security taxes. They also govern the withholding federal income taxes and Medicare taxes from each employee's paycheck.

Remember you will not need this number if you choose to be a sole proprietorship for your business. It is simple to apply, either you can do it yourself or get your accountant to apply for you, but the process is simple, you fill out the form SS-4, which can be filed online, via Fax or via mail.

Here is a link to IRS website where you can download or fill out the form online. https://www.irs.gov/businesses/small-businesses-self-employed/how-to-apply-for-an-ein

Form SS-4

Form SS-4
(Rev. January 2010)
Department of the Treasury
Internal Revenue Service

Application for Employer Identification Number

(For use by employers, corporations, partnerships, trusts, estates, churches, government agencies, Indian tribal entities, certain individuals, and others.)

► See separate instructions for each line.   ► Keep a copy for your records.

OMB No. 1545-0003

EIN

Type or print clearly.

1	Legal name of entity (or individual) for whom the EIN is being requested

2 Trade name of business (if different from name on line 1)	3 Executor, administrator, trustee, "care of" name

4a Mailing address (room, apt., suite no. and street, or P.O. box)	5a Street address (if different) (Do not enter a P.O. box.)
4b City, state, and ZIP code (if foreign, see instructions)	5b City, state, and ZIP code (if foreign, see instructions)

6 County and state where principal business is located

7a Name of responsible party	7b SSN, ITIN, or EIN

8a Is this application for a limited liability company (LLC) (or a foreign equivalent)? . . . . ☐ Yes ☐ No
8b If 8a is "Yes," enter the number of LLC members . . . . . ►

8c If 8a is "Yes," was the LLC organized in the United States? . . . . ☐ Yes ☐ No

9a Type of entity (check only one box). Caution. If 8a is "Yes," see the instructions for the correct box to check.

☐ Sole proprietor (SSN) _____
☐ Partnership
☐ Corporation (enter form number to be filed) ► _____
☐ Personal service corporation
☐ Church or church-controlled organization
☐ Other nonprofit organization (specify) ► _____
☐ Other (specify) ► _____

☐ Estate (SSN of decedent) _____
☐ Plan administrator (TIN) _____
☐ Trust (TIN of grantor) _____
☐ National Guard   ☐ State/local government
☐ Farmers' cooperative   ☐ Federal government/military
☐ REMIC   ☐ Indian tribal governments/enterprises
Group Exemption Number (GEN) if any ►

9b If a corporation, name the state or foreign country (if applicable) where incorporated

State	Foreign country

10 Reason for applying (check only one box)
☐ Started new business (specify type) ► _____
☐ Hired employees (Check the box and see line 13.)
☐ Compliance with IRS withholding regulations
☐ Other (specify) ►

☐ Banking purpose (specify purpose) ► _____
☐ Changed type of organization (specify new type) ► _____
☐ Purchased going business
☐ Created a trust (specify type) ► _____
☐ Created a pension plan (specify type) ► _____

11 Date business started or acquired (month, day, year). See instructions.	12 Closing month of accounting year
13 Highest number of employees expected in the next 12 months (enter -0- if none). If no employees expected, skip line 14.	14 If you expect your employment tax liability to be $1,000 or less in a full calendar year and want to file Form 944 annually instead of Forms 941 quarterly, check here. (Your employment tax liability generally will be $1,000 or less if you expect to pay $4,000 or less in total wages.) If you do not check this box, you must file Form 941 for every quarter. ☐

Agricultural	Household	Other

15 First date wages or annuities were paid (month, day, year). Note. If applicant is a withholding agent, enter date income will first be paid to nonresident alien (month, day, year) . . . . ►

16 Check one box that best describes the principal activity of your business.
☐ Construction ☐ Rental & leasing ☐ Transportation & warehousing ☐ Accommodation & food service ☐ Wholesale-other ☐ Retail
☐ Real estate ☐ Manufacturing ☐ Finance & insurance ☐ Other (specify) ►
☐ Health care & social assistance ☐ Wholesale-agent/broker

17 Indicate principal line of merchandise sold, specific construction work done, products produced, or services provided.

18 Has the applicant entity shown on line 1 ever applied for and received an EIN? ☐ Yes ☐ No
If "Yes," write previous EIN here ►

Third Party Designee	Complete this section only if you want to authorize the named individual to receive the entity's EIN and answer questions about the completion of this form.	
	Designee's name	Designee's telephone number (include area code)
	Address and ZIP code	Designee's fax number (include area code)

Under penalties of perjury, I declare that I have examined this application, and to the best of my knowledge and belief, it is true, correct, and complete.

Name and title (type or print clearly) ►

Applicant's telephone number (include area code)

Applicant's fax number (include area code)

The Bureau of Alcohol, Tobacco, and Firearms

BATF, a division of the US Treasury, is the body of government you will deal with if you serve alcoholic beverages.

They require a Special Occupational Tax Stamp. The stamp is not a federal license but a receipt for the payment you make.

State and local governments essentially control your liquor license, renewals, and laws.

 **Local Laws**

Local laws ensure that you are operating a fair and safe restaurant. Exact rules and enforcement differ from city-to-city and state-to-state.

Health Department

Govern what you eat, serve.

Sanitary rules for food safety and sanitation parameters.

Good for 1 year at a time.

Can be revoked at any time.

State and local Health Departments work together administering inspections and licenses.

Fire Department

Issues fire permits.

State fire marshal and local fire department administer regulations and guidelines.

Must follow the National Fire Protection Code.

Building Department

Issues building permits.	
Performs inspections.	
Building codes differ within communities.	
May have to deal with several building permits and occupancy certificates.	

ADDITIONAL AGENCIES TO CONFORM WITH

Signage Commission	Controls features of signage and permits.
Water and Sewer Commission	Determines septic system rules and water supply guidelines.
Americans with Disabilities Act	Checks that disability and wheelchair

(ADA)	requirements are met.

Dairy Commission	Often operates within the Health Department.

U.S. Department of Agriculture Department of Homeland Security	Regulate safety of food supplies.

Secretary of State	Must approve and register your business name.

OPENING A COMMERCIAL BANK ACCOUNT

This is one important step, but it can only be done after you have a fully executed article of incorporation which has been approved by the state, and you have an EIN number assigned by the IRS.

Once you have these two documents, you should be able to go to a bank and open your first commercial bank account.

But remember to check and understand various types of commercial checking account fees, you want to find a bank that offers free or almost free commercial checking account because some larger banks can charge you hundreds of dollars each month depending on how many transactions you do.

Make sure to ask and shop around before you sign on the dotted line.

COSTS TO OPEN A RESTAURANT

Depending on Restaurant size and type of Restaurant you open. Or existing building.

150,000	**Site build out, signage parking lot, HVAC, rest rooms, kitchen design, configuration**
300,000	**Industrial cooking and ventilation equipment, freezers, refrigerators, stools, tables for cutting and prep work, counters, cooling stations, shelving**
125,000	**Dining room furniture glassware, silverware, etc.**
8,000	**First-year insurance no vehicles**

75,000	First-year wages not including you

50,000	First-year rent at $4,000 a month
4,000	Security deposit
	Versus buy which may have gov't impact fees of $20,000 to $120,000

30,000	First three months of food and beverage

Continued

12,000	Marketing, fliers, coupons, advertising, PR
10,000	Opening event

5,000	Licenses and permits

8,000	Menus, depending on type of restaurant.

Vary	Accounting costs
15,000	POS

792,000	Total

Let's look at some realities. The costs are determined by the size and location of your restaurant. Variables for the number of seats would be either increased or decreased wages, dining furniture, fixtures, and food costs.

If you were to purchase or lease an existing restaurant, renovations for a similar layout might cost less because you are buying the build out in your price. The rent, however, will be higher.

These decisions require the help of financial and accounting experts. If you are not an expert, you need help. What is not covered in the above are ongoing costs like utilities, trash, garbage and grease disposal.

Accommodations for these should be in your build out, and, of course, necessary to open for business. Ongoing costs in your overhead will be part of your yearly operating costs and included in your business plan.

Renovating an existing restaurant with a similar concept will cost less, though the rent may be comparatively higher because the value of the previous build-out is already in the purchase/rental price.

Various stations in the restaurant kitchen keep work organized and running smoothly. You may need stations with special equipment or just a few stations based on your menu, space, and budget.

For instance, a sauté station used for the most complicated dishes. This area requires a skilled cook. This station should also allow enough room for cooking several items at once and include a prep area. You need a multi-burner gas range and cooking equipment.

A grill station, which also requires a skilled cook, is a flattop or char-broiler for cooking meats. Required cooking equipment and possibly a prep area is needed.

Others are a fry station, a wait station and possibly salad, dessert and pizza stations.
Servers pick up food from the kitchen line. There may be more than one kitchen line, and they are attended by someone acting as an expeditor. Garnishes, plates, heating lamps, etc. should all be included.

You can see from the above that restaurant equipment includes dining furniture to ice cream machines, commercial ovens to dishes, freezers to prep areas. Suppliers can be of some help. Research each company before you use them, and be careful of higher pricing tactics,

Maybe all your equipment doesn't have to be new. You may be able to find excellent used equipment.

Tableware is a viable candidate for purchasing used and saving money. The key is that you purchase items that match your theme and décor. Second-hand utensils, glasses, dishes, tables, and chairs can work as well.

They should be in perfect condition; restaurant dishes and utensils are different. Budget and durability will rule here. Dishes are often handled, sometimes roughly and may be washed numerous times a day.

Bigger pieces of restaurant equipment such as refrigerators, ovens, stove and fry units can be found as used equipment or leased.

▶▶❙ CRUNCH THOSE NUMBERS ❙◀◀

There are pros and cons to buying new and buying used. Buying used equipment.

Pros

- Save money that can be put towards food cost, insurance or marketing.
- Because of the high rate of failed restaurants, used equipment is often in good condition and sometimes so new the warranty is still attached.
- Prices are negotiable. Haggle with dealers, go to auctions.
- Ask for freebies to be tossed in with your purchase such as mixer or prep table.

Cons

- Warranties may be expired. You purchase used equipment in an 'as is' condition. However, commercial equipment is so durable, parts can often be replaced to sustain huge savings.
- It's a gamble. If your used equipment breaks beyond repair or its repairs are too costly, you have spent a lot of money that goes out the door. Then you will spend more money for replacement equipment.

- A ray of sunshine. Some items have a good chance of working for prolonged periods of time.
- Commercial grade ovens and gas ranges have long life spans in the restaurant environment. Electric, not good. Electric models take too long to heat up and cool down and have a lot of parts that can break.
- Commercial gas fryers are good used purchases. Buyer beware. Check to see the instructions on changing the oil and calibrations are included.

Compare new-to-used-to leased. Compare prices as long-term investments and amortization for taxes. Equipment better suited for monthly leasing are those with a short restaurant lifespan. Additionally, some equipment like coffee machines are free if you buy certain products exclusively.

Unexpected Costs
One of the biggest reasons so many restaurants fail is due to lack of planning for unexpected roadblocks. In other words, undercapitalized.

Knowledge is power. Do your research, and talk to people that will help you understand road blocks and other possibilities you need to prepare for.

It is estimated that about 80% of restaurants fail because they misjudged the capital needed to start up. Expect the unexpected. Wait times for equipment delivery, wrong delivery, lost equipment, plumber's schedules, finding dreadful things behind the walls, parking lot, and restroom problems.

The budget for situations like these. It's hard to estimate, it's hard to know. But, something will happen, so make your best estimate to cover some worse case scenarios.

A rule of thumb: After you get all final quotes from general contractors, and crunch the numbers, add 10%.

A sample of some overlooked expenses. These can determine your failure or success.

- Money for financial deposits. For instance, have enough cash to pre-pay for services such as utilities. Telephone companies, internet, linen providers, etc. Especially when you are new many providers want deposits or cash up front.

- Remember your concept? Your theme and your look are all reflected in the design of your restaurant. Including outdoor signage, maybe uniforms, and interior design features. Go the extra mile to be consistent.

- Maybe into the project you don't like the fabrics, window treatments, whatever and realize you need to upgrade. There are going to be things that, once seen in real-life, just don't work for your design.

- Construction or structure bombshells. These setbacks could include rewiring, additional electric or phone accommodations. Relocating equipment.

Small changes, big changes, and change of mind will quickly add up. Think about your walk-through and punch list. Sometimes things don't show up until then. Plus, licensing agents may have some new challenges for you. These surprises don't show up in new construction exclusively. Beware when renting or purchasing an existing restaurant or building you will be converting.

- Who is running the show? Is it always the chef, or a joint effort? For instance, a chef who wants organic, farm to table or imported, hard to get supplies could result in an expensive change from how you first developed your menu. You need to decide if changes are a preference or judicious.

This applies to equipment, as well. Additional or rearranging equipment based on "I forgot!" or chef requirements can get into thousands of dollar changes.

Consideration would be to confer with your chef first. You've got your menu and theme down, you might want to develop menus with your chef. Maybe (s)he is your first hire. Or, hire one as a consultant.

- The full cost of food also presents challenges. New restaurant owners often undercapitalized how much it costs to put food on a plate. For instance, a sandwich shop, deli, diner no matter what needs condiments, paper wrapping and containers for to-go, or the cost of plastic plates and utensils. Maybe even the cost of self-service trays.

A hamburger needs a bun, toppings, fries, condiments, and napkins. You can calculate these costs as you develop your menu. However, what if you change the menu?

Costs developed based on your opening menu may change. Menu changes might need new equipment.

A rule of thumb: After you open, a minimal of 25% will have to be changed, fine-tuned or adjusted based on your customers.

- The ambiance is often a forgotten feature. Music lends to the ambiance and theme of your restaurant. Fine dining, casual and ethnic restaurants depend on it.

  Music licensing is required. As a significant feature for creating mood and ambiance, you are lawfully required to carry the proper licenses that regulate the entertainment industries' copy write laws.

  Several Performing Rights Organizations (PROs) work with restaurants, TV, radio, anywhere music is played in the public domain, to protect intellectual property. i.e., songwriters, musicians, artists.

A license for TV in your restaurant or bar is also required. About $1,000, depending on your situation. Exempt is a TV in your employee's lounge, your office, away from any public domain.

- Remember our McDonald's friend who put staff at the outside ordering lines with tablets? That may be a training cost, plus other costs to get all your staff ready for opening day.

  Now, our friend at McDonald's probably took his cost out of profits. You won't have any yet. Expert staff needs training, just like the franchises provide. Who by the way, if you remember, send staff to a three-week training.

- There will be miscellaneous expenses you can't possibly think of ahead of time. For instance, trips to the hardware store, DIY big-box stores, providing dinner for overtime staff preparing for opening.

Carpet nails, window, and door insulation strips. Broken locks, etc. Business cards, office supplies, office furniture.

A rule of thumb: you don't know what some of these miscellaneous expenses will be. Make the best estimate or guess that you can, then double it.

WRITING THE RIGHT BUSINESS PLAN

 A business plan is two things:

📍 A roadmap to the success of your restaurant focused on reaching your financial and personal goals.

📍 A road map to obtaining financing, persuading others to invest in your dream.

Writing a business plan sounds like a daunting task, but it shouldn't be. Just be clear and concise. Keep it short. No one is going to read hundreds of pages that you have slaved over. Start with a cover page followed by a Table of Contents then go on from there.

Business plans will vary by the type of restaurant you are planning.

Here is a sample of an Executive Summary, the first section of your business plan, provided by Bplans.

Many examples following the Executive Summary are also from Bplans. This is an excellent source of free information and templates. On the open web and quoted here, they also recommend LivePlan for any graphics you need.

These are excellent places to start and represent two of the top leaders in the industry providing such valuable information.

Using any free information from the internet does not necessarily preclude you from using a professional. Perhaps you do the hard work and have a professional review it, give you input and advice. Your banker or other investors may help as well.

EXECUTIVE SUMMARY

Gabri's Lounge & Restaurant is a 60 seat fine-dining restaurant with a 20-seat lounge. We focus on our New American-Swedish menu with a touch of Asian influence.

We will be located in the booming, and rapidly expanding, borough of Long Branch, New Jersey 'on the shore.'

The outlook for the future of Long Branch is promising. Developers are recreating a $150 million first-class resort project. The old pier will be rebuilt with ferry service to Manhattan, New York City, beach cabanas, boardwalk and a bike path over a total of 25 acres. There will be 100,000 sq. ft. of commercial space, and over 700 residential units with condo and townhouses ranging from $200,000-$500,000; rentals from $1000-$2,500 a month, and a two-tier garage. The combination of these elements will provide the city with a year-round economy.

The area is in need of a warm and friendly place with excellent food. A place where you always know you will get the best of everything. Gabri's Lounge & Restaurant will feature a cozy dining room and an elegant lounge. Comfortable furnishings and decor with soothing warm tones. The lounge has comfy couches and antique love seats with a softly lit bar. It will be the perfect place to stop in for a bite to eat, for a drink or for a small business meeting. For extra comfort and to please a large group of people we will make up special hors d' oeuvre platters for customers.

The menu will be inspired from different countries' specialties and appeal to a diverse clientele. You can get Swedish specialties like herring, gravlax, and meatballs, or you can go a little bit more International and choose a red curry chicken with basmati rice, or an Asian grilled shrimp with spinach, tofu and black bean sauce. We will also have a special pasta dish entree every day plus the 'all American meal' such as barbecue beef ribs and baked beans. Adding value will be an interesting business lunch menu with specialties every day. The menu will change every 3-4 months but keep the favorites. Prices will be competitive with other upscale restaurants in the area. However, it is the strategy of Gabri's Lounge & Restaurant to give a perception of higher value than its competitors, through its food, service, and entertainment.

The lounge and restaurant will be open seven days a week. We will offer special theme nights to attract new customers to Gabri's. The restaurant will be fine dining in a cozy atmosphere. Warm colors, fresh flowers, soft music, candles and amazing artwork from some of the area's most notable new artists. This will contribute to a sense of community and give new artists a chance to show their work for a diverse clientele. During the busy summer months, you can also sit outside on our patio, and we will offer a special summer menu, featuring lighter fare, exotic drinks, as well as non-alcoholic offerings. The patio and garden setting will be a fun and casual atmosphere for the summer crowd.

The service will be relaxed, very friendly and correct. We will hire the best people available, training, motivating and encourage them, and thereby retaining the friendliest most efficient staff possible. Our management team is comprised of individuals whose backgrounds consist of 50 years' experience in food, restaurant, and hotel, catering, management, finance, marketing, art and motion pictures.

Catering will be a major part of the business. "Leave it to Linda Catering" already has an established clientele and we are growing each and every day. We feel in today's hectic work schedule customers don't always have time to set up that birthday party or another event that we all need and want.
Now customers can leave it to pros and get the finest, most memorable party or dinner ever. We have years of experience in the catering business and know what an important client wants and needs. We will have a large International menu for customers to select from, and we will offer full catering service providing everything from table settings to the dessert. We anticipate our total sales allocation to be 85% restaurant sales and 15%

catering sales. The combined cost of sales will be 33% producing a gross profit of 67% on total sales.

Most important to us is our financial success, and we believe this will be achieved by offering high-quality service and excellent food with an interesting twist. We have created financial projections based on our experience and knowledge of the area. With a start-up expenditure of $385,000, we can generate $1,085,465 in sales by the end of year two, and produce good net profits by the end of year three.

We are seeking an SBA 7(A) loan guaranty for $200,000 with a 7% interest rate. We are investing $60,000 of our own capital and seeking to raise an additional $125,000 from investors. Our preferred instrument will be five-year subordinated notes with an attractive coupon rate of 12% for the first two years and 15% for the remaining three years. At the end of five years, the investors' notes will have matured, and original principal plus a 2% premium and the final interest payment will be made. Our investment philosophy is conservative. Since restaurant start-ups are so speculative, our belief and commitment to our investors will be to pay a generous, predictable rate of return while not strangling our operational cash flow. As our business becomes more established and reliable, our ability to pay an improved return of capital will be evidenced by an increased coupon rate of 15% of original principal. At maturity, we feel it proper to retire the notes with a 2% premium to original principal invested.

Gabri's Executive Summary is a bit hard to read. You want to tell a story, your readers and potential investors want to hear your story, but write it in an easy to read format.

Shorter paragraphs, for instance, and fewer passive sentences. Also, spell-check and proofread your summary. The Gabri's summary is being quoted here, word for word.

The rest of your business plan includes various parts of the following. The final amount of material you write should be governed by the size and type of your restaurant.

1.0 Executive Summary (example above)

1.1 Mission

1.2 Objectives

1.3 Keys to Success

2.0 Company Summary

2.1 Company Ownership

2.2 Start-up Summary

Gabri's start-up summary costs:

Start-up requirements

Start-up Funding	
Start-up Expenses to Fund	$300,000
Start-up Assets to Fund	$85,000
Total Funding Required	$385,000
Assets	
Non-cash Assets from Start-up	$0
Cash Requirements from Start-up	$85,000
Additional Cash Raised	$0

Cash Balance on Starting Date	$85,000
Total Assets	$85,000
Liabilities and Capital	
Liabilities	
Current Borrowing	$0
Long-term Liabilities	$200,000
Accounts Payable (Outstanding Bills)	$0
Other Current Liabilities (interest-free)	$0
Total Liabilities	$200,000
Capital	
Planned Investment	
John & Linda	$60,000
Investor 2	$25,000
Investor 3	$50,000
Investor 4	$50,000
Additional Investment Requirement	$0
Total Planned Investment	$185,000
Loss at Start-up (Start-up Expenses)	($300,000)
Total Capital	($115,000)
Total Capital and Liabilities	$85,000
Total Funding	$385,000

Gabri's funding submission:

Start-up expenses

Legal	$5,000
Stationery & Sign	$5,000
Office Supplies (Computer, Fax, Printer)	$5,000
Uniforms	$2,000
Insurance	$2,000
Rent & Security Deposit	$18,000
Outdoor Patio & Garden Setting	$10,000
Liquor License	$75,000
Furniture	$40,000
Cash Register/Software	$10,000
Bathrooms Repair (Materials/Labor)	$15,000
Windows Repair (Materials/Labor)	$5,000
Floor & Wall Coverings (Materials/Labor)	$20,000
Paint	$4,000
Lighting & Lamps (Materials/Labor)	$12,000
Phone & Gas Deposit	$1,000

Food & Liquor	$30,000
Kitchen Supplies	$30,000
Music/Stereo/TV	$4,000
Cleaning	$1,000
High Chair & Booster Seat	$200
Advertising & Website	$5,800
Total Start-up Expenses	$300,000
Start-up Assets	
Cash Required	$85,000
Other Current Assets	$0
Long-term Assets	$0
Total Assets	$85,000
Total Requirements	$385,000

Your Business Plan Continues with:

3.0 Services

3.1 Pricing and Profitability

4.0 Market Analysis Summary

4.1 Market Segmentation

4.2 Target Market Segment Strategy

5.0 Strategy and Implementation Summary

8.7 Exit Strategy

9.0 Sample Menus

10.0 Appendix

The appendix on the Bplan website is filled with dozens of financial sheets. Look on their site to obtain free examples, numbers, and directions.

(I included a sample business plan at the end of this book from bplans.com. they are the ultimate authority in creating the best and most professional business plans. If you need a solid and accurate business plan, visit http://www.bplans.com I highly recommend it)

GETTING A BANK TO FINANCE YOUR RESTAURANT

What are your options for getting financing to open and run your restaurant? How much financing do you need for your restaurant type?

Financing is not just a one-time deal. There are three steps of financing that you need.

1. **Seed Capital**

   This is money for start-up, preparing your restaurant for opening followed by operating costs for a period of time before profits are made.

2. **Growth Capital**

   Funds to grow your business once you have proven it is a feasible concept and you are up and running.

3. Harvest Cash

This is cash needed for when a partner, investor, or an owner wants their money out of the restaurant.

You have all this information built into your business plan. You need to have money for any of the above events six to nine months before it's needed.

Your seed capital or start-up is what you need to open. What are you going to put in your business plan? $80,000, $550,000, a million? Once you have determined what you need, don't undersell yourself. You may think asking for less will make it easier to get approved. Don't risk it.

Also, your banker or investor will need to see the use of these funds outlined in your business plan. For instance, do you need it all at once? Can a percentage be available but not drawn on until another stage?

For instance, your growth capital stage. These funds will be needed when you require a cash injection to continue growth to the point of stable profit-making. You will also need a line of credit. Here's how that works. You project $80,000 in sales per month and want to have a two-month safety net of $160,000 cash. This is funding you will need to get from your banker as a line of credit. It serves as a safety net for start-ups.

The first source of capital is often the restaurant owner's own resources. Mortgages, IRAs, etc. After personal assets, an Angel Investor is the most common source of funds.

An Angel Investor is a private investor that will want a business plan, objectives, goals, strategy and projections before meeting with you.

They will also more than likely want a stake in your restaurant in exchange for their investment. Angel investors are the largest source of capital in the U.S. You can find them in investment clubs, and venture capitalist groups. Their trade group is called the Angel Capital Association.

You always have the option of funding via a partnership. However, at this point in the game you would have already set-up the legal structure of your business and have resolved any investment issues with a partner.

Next, are banks, who are not always favorable towards start-ups. They get more interested when you need growth infusions of cash, buy-outs, and lines of credit because you have already proven yourself.

Banks do, however, have guidelines on how they will may approve your loan.

First is your character. Are you respected and well known? Can you pay the monthly loan payment? Your restaurant and equipment will be collateral but what else do you have?

How is your credit? Is your business plan clear, concise and feasible? Have you included realistic cash flow projections? Do you have the research and data to back-up what you are selling to them?

A banker wants to see a well-thought-out business plan, written by you, using your business experience and skills. Bankers are not crazy about plans for your restaurant that someone else has written.

That doesn't mean not getting the professional help you may need. What it means is that you better know your plan inside and out, can prove it and prove yourself to be capable.

Another funding alternative is the commercial finance companies. They typically have high-interest rates but are more likely to finance your start-up. In return, your interest rate will be anywhere from three to seven percent above prime.

The Small Business Administration (SBA) works with commercial lenders and will guarantee a loan up to

90%. They do, however, consider restaurants a substantial risk.

Again, a lot rides on your experience, skill, business acumen and a complete business plan when talking with the SBA.

Research who you will get a loan from as carefully as you have researched the rest of your dream

First, come up with a list of banks you want to apply to. It is not a good idea to apply at multiple banks at once. Instead, come up with a list of say, four banks, go and talk in depth with their business loan department and find out their full requirements.

In my experience, I have noticed typically smaller local banks are more inclined to offer loans to local small businesses such as restaurants, gas stations, and laundromats than some of the bigger banks. But that may not be true for every part of the country, so it is best to talk to at least 3-4 banks and try to get the feel if they are really into this sort of business financing or not before you submit your application.

Sometimes your local business brokers or commercial real estate agents can guide you to the right bank, as they often deal with similar situations and know which banks are more favorable to these sort of loans. You can also ask your bank that you deal with everyday and ask their advice.

Once you narrow down to 2 banks, make trips to meet their loan officer and see what their requirements are. Just remember, every bank will have similar requirements, but they can still vary widely based on many factors, like how much down payment they require and how much collateral they need from you, even if they offer some SBA assisted loans or not. Your goal would be to deal with a bank that offers SBA loans. SBA stands for Small Business Administration. SBA is a federal government agency whose primary goal is to help small business owners get financing.

Here is SBA website where you can read about their newest small business loan programs.
www.SBA.Gov

Most times the SBA offers some sort of guarantee (50-80%) on your behalf to the bank, so banks are somewhat more lenient in approving the loan as they are not in the risk for the total amount they are giving you. But the downside to this is the amount of paperwork you have to furnish is monumental in most cases.

The SBA's requirements can be broad and extensive, so be prepared to gather up a lot of paperwork.

Another drawback to an SBA loan is it can take up to 6 months to get approval from them. They run slower than most banks and, in their defense, they do have a lot of applicants that are submitting applications, so they have to go through all that, and it is always first come first served, so be patient.

But if you have a larger down payment (say 30% or higher) or have some good collateral to offer then you can opt out on SBA loans and get most any banks to offer you a conventional loan. Provided you have all your ducks in a row like your credit is in excellent shape, your tax returns show good incomes for previous years and so on so forth.

When you talk to any banks, they will hand you something called a loan package. Most times the package will have a checklist of documents that they want you to furnish to them along with a loan application and some other waiver forms, depending on your bank.

One thing to keep in mind: all banks and commercial lenders do have to follow certain guidelines that are set by federal and state banking authorities. Also, every bank will look at something called the LTV (Loan to Value) ratio of the property or business you are looking to buy. LTV is essentially where banks look at the actual value of the business you are looking to buy and how much of that value they can loan you.

But in any case, let's look at the list of documents you will need to get ready to submit to your bank. Some of these items I will mention here may not be on your bank's checklist but do gather them anyway as it will make you look more professional and business-like.

First The Items You Will Need From The Seller For This Loan Process:

- Last two years of P&L
- Last three years Tax Returns of the business
- A balance sheet
- Any and all health and equipment inspection reports and repair estimates

Now Here Is What You Need To Gather:

1. You need to get copies of at least last 3 years of tax returns. Make sure the copies are signed.

2. Your resume (they may not even ask you for it, but remember the person that may approve your loan may never meet you but this way at least he or she gets to see who you are and how qualified you are. It always helps)

3. Copy of your Corp. Articles, (yes, you have to get this done before you even apply for your loan.)

4. Personal financial statement for all Corp. Officers or members (See Appendix B for a sample). Make sure to sign it. If you are married and file joint tax returns than your wife needs to have one prepared for her as well, or you can make a joint personal financial statement for both of you and make sure you both sign that document.

5. Copy of the commercial appraisal (if applicable)

6. Copy of signed purchase agreement and Letter of Intent (if buying an existing restaurant)

7. Copy of your EIN (Employer's Identification Number) issued by the IRS

8. Copy of all member/partner's Driver's licenses and social security cards

9. A well thought out and expertly written Business Plan (not a store bought one or copy-pasted one; one that is written for that specific business. Get help if you need to, but this has to be a well thought out plan. Do it as your life depends on it. Trust me on this.)

10. Last but not least, the loan application all filled out. Use a computer and printer if possible. If not, write very clearly, so it is easy to read.

11. A cover letter addressed to the loan Dept. where you describe what is in the package and thanking them for reviewing your loan application. Lastly, tell them where they can find you if they need further

help or additional documents from you. It just makes you look more professional

Now, remember to organize these papers with nice tabs and in a binding folder where anyone can open the folder, look at the tab and go directly to that specific section.

If you are applying for a SBA-specific business loan, then SBA may also give you a loan package with some more documents and forms to fill out.

HIRING STAFF

Labor costs and food are the two biggest expenses in operating a restaurant. This section covers the staff you will need to open your restaurant, which is typically or upward of 25% of your expenses.

The areas to address in labor costs are hiring, improving staff quality, scheduling staff efficiently and cross-training staff.

Staff efficiency is calculations. Start with the number of tables used for each service. Mix your staffs' level of experience for each daypart. For instance, you need quick wait staff during certain parts of the day. Mix them in with rookies instead of all rookies, so the dining room doesn't come to a standstill.

For non-table service restaurants, determining how many customers you will have for each daypart calculates number of employees needed during those times. There will always be pre-opening and post-closing staff needed for various duties.

Cross-training means getting the most productivity you can from each employee. For instance, slow service may cause people to leave and not return. Bus staff and managers could serve diners. Prep cooks could help prepare more food items that are on the menu.

Improving staff quality is a make or break exercise. Since all restaurants rely on repeat business, don't pay dining room staff the least amount. Poor customer service and staff turnover are too frequent. Put your money to pay for the reasons for customers will return.

Get top-quality experienced and trained staff who know how to sell specials, upsell items and work with the kitchen to get orders in and out as quickly as possible.

Use websites like Restaurant Owner.com and others for extensive information on hiring staff. Many have job descriptions and applications that are free and can be customized with your restaurant name and logo.

Training programs and manuals are also available from many companies' and their websites. Take advantage of free materials and your ability to research. A lot of different talent is required to run a restaurant.

Front of restaurant   Maître de
    Servers

Bartender   Kitchen manager

    Line cook and prep

Bussers   Dishwashers

You may need additional staff, less or just different. Staff required is based on the type of restaurant you open, size, hours of operations and number of amenities you offer. Now let's discuss how to find and hire the right people.

HOW TO FIND AND HIRE THE RIGHT PEOPLE

I broke this staffing part into a 10 step process, and I will discuss each in detail.

1. WHERE AND HOW TO FIND THE RIGHT PEOPLE TO HIRE?

Best practices to hire good people are through advertising in a way that covers your city or locality and not just in your neighborhood.

I have three suggestions on where to advertise and find people

A. Run an ad on Craigslist, you may be surprised how often people look for jobs on craigslist, craigslist is an essential tool for lot of things, from selling your old couch and bicycle to hiring people to do your yard or carpentry work to hiring new employees. I use Craigslist every time I need help, I even hired a great bookkeeper from there.

B. Word of mouth. You can ask some of your other employees if they know of any good and decent person they can recommend. Ask your friends, or other business owners that you know well, this way you at least have a reference where they are coming from.

C. Hiring employees from other local retailers, sounds bad I know but again remember you are not doing anything illegal or unethical, let me explain- you go to your local burger joint and the lady that took your order was very courteous and professional. Strike up a conversation with her, compliment on her fessionalism, let her know you own such and such business, and you are looking to hire some good and decent employees. Ask her if she knows anyone that she can recommend. Give her your business card. You will see that out of five people you meet this way three will call you either with a recommendation, or they will call to apply for themselves. There are three reasons she may contact you, one: obviously people love compliments, second most employees do not feel appreciated enough at their current jobs. 3rd, everyone wants to move up at their job and eventually make more money. So take advantage of that.

Now that you have some applicants calling you, you need to give them each an application right? Where do you get these job applications? I am sure you can go to the local office supply store and pick a stack of them up but is that a good idea? The answer is No; those applications are very generic and not designed for your type of business. So its best to create one or modify an existing one you may already have that fits your needs. You can also go to restaurantowner.com and create one like I mentioned earlier.

When preparing a job application few things to keep in mind:

Absolutely no mention of the social security number on the application.

It is also a good idea not to ask about race in a job application

Make sure to ask about their education level and previous employment history along with how many addresses they have lived in last five years. These three things can tell you a lot about a person. If an applicant held one job for last 5 years, lived in one address in that 5 years and has high school education, chances are he or she will be a good employee, compare to if an applicant had 4 jobs in last 5 years, moved 3 times in that same period and did not have a high school diploma.

When asking about previous employments, make sure to ask the name and contact information of the company along with the name of their supervisors. This way you can check their references. Remember it is a common practice for employers not to reveal any details of a current or former employee, so if you ask were they good or bad at their job, you may not get an answer, you may just have to read (hear in this case) between the lines. But they all can say if that person can be rehired or not. Your answer lies in that answer if they say he or she is can be rehired; you know they are saying they do recommend that person.

2. ASKING THE RIGHT QUESTION DURING INTERVIEW

Once you find some good application, call a few of them for an interview, I always give them a simple math test to see if they can calculate basic add and subtract in their head. It is a good idea to ask a few hypothetical questions ranging from how to handle a customer service issue to an emergency situation like if someone ought to get sick inside what and how they would handle that emergency. Watch and listen and see if they use a commonsense approach to answering them or not. Then I ask them if they have any physical limitation which may prevent them from performing the normal duties and responsibilities of a restauarnt job.

Next I usually ask if they can bring a background check of themselves from the local police dept, and I do offer to pay for that cost. It saves money and time to have them provide you with that report instead of you running a background check on them. Once all these things check off, go ahead and hire them. One more thing to make clear right before you hire them, do let them know that it is your company policy to hire people with a 60 days probation period. Meaning they can be let go in this 60 days anytime without giving them any reasons based on their performance.

Once you get the background check back, provided it is doable in your city and state, you hire them; there are some basic paperwork that you need to give them to fill out. I am sure everyone of you that is in this business have a set of paperwork that you give your new hire. But I would still like to go through a checklist of some paperwork I give to my new hires so you can match them with yours.

A. Completed job Application that you already have
B. W2 from IRS
C. New hire Handbook (If you are a franchise, your company usually provide you with some basic new hire training material to hand out to each new hire, or you can get one from restaurantowner.com)
D. A disclaimer about the 60-day probation period (Where I explain for next 60 days they are on probation, and their job can be terminated based on poor performance, I have them sign it)
E. Their criminal background check paper that brought to you keep it in their personnel file
F. Copy of their Social security and Driver's license

Remember some states require you to register all new employees you hire with the DOL(Dept. of Labor) within seven days of hiring, if not there will be a fine imposed on you. So check with your state's DOL and see if they require it. One more thing you need to find out about your state is if your state is an employer at will state or not.

Alabama among many other states is an employer at will state. Meaning you can terminate anyone anytime without giving them any reason. Yes, sounds odd I know and maybe I am oversimplifying it, but the essence is that you really do not have to give them much of a reason for the termination.

3. PROVIDING PROPER TRAINING

Once you hire an employee, it is important to provide them with proper training. First give them a walk around the restaurant and the kitchen and show them how the whole process works, then explain their job duties and responsibilities, like what is expected of them before they start their shift and after they close their shifts. I usually provide three full days of training before I let any new employee working or running a shift all by themselves.

4. EMPLOYEE APPEARANCE

Appearance is the most important first impression on your customer; you do not get a 2nd chance to create that first impression, so make sure your employees are in uniform.

One quick note on that, if you don't have a logo for your restaurant, you can go online to Fivver.com and pay $5 and get a logo created for you. So no reason not to be professional and making sure your restaurant and employees look just as much professional as big name restaurant chain employees.

5. MOTIVATING AND EMPOWERING YOUR EMPLOYEES

You need to make sure your employees do not feel that this is a dead end job. in order to do so, you need to motivate them. Typically there are three ways that you can motivate your employees.

A. By showing them the ladder they can climb to be in management one day. Show them how someone can go from a waiter to shift leader, to shift manager to assistant manager and then finally store manager one day. Let them know that it is possible with hard work and dedication.

B. Tell them how to give our raises to your employees. I typically tell all new hire that I would start them at a certain hourly rate then after 60 days they will get a raise to certain hourly rate and every 6 months I will do a performance review of them and if I see they are performing well, they will get a raise.

C. Another great way to motivate your staff is just simply by telling them they are doing a great job, give them compliment when you see a good work, acknowledge it and show them you noticed. A simple "thank you" a petting on the back can go a long way sometimes. Remember everybody wants to feel appreciated.

6. TEACHING THEM MARKETING 101

In this step, your team needs to know your marketing strategy so they can promote your restaurant. Let me explain, even though most restaurants show their specials right on top of the menu or display it right on the table, I strongly believe mentioning it by name and explaining how and why it is such a great special makes customers more incline to opt in. The power of face to face marketing can be a very powerful thing.

7. REWARDING THE RIGHT BEHAVIOR

If you see an employee did a great job handling a bad situation at work, or they showed some exceptional quality or ability which is beyond their daily work duties and responsibilities, reward them by at least acknowledge their work or effort. Buy them lunch or have lunch with them, it can mean a lot to them. Give them a gift certificate for a movie or a pizza, this can make them feel appreciated and proud of being a part of your team.

8. HOW TO DISCIPLINE BAD BEHAVIOR

Now let's face the truth, we don't always get the best employees, there are bad apples in every bunch right? Now how do you discipline a bad behavior when you see one, it could be that someone is not doing their job properly, or giving poor customer service to not doing their side work or even for showing up work late more than once in the same week. Nothing too serious or major.

Let me just say here if you see a truly bad behavior or violation of your company policy by an employee or even subordination where you asked them to perform a duty, and they refuse, these are the grounds for immediate termination and no other disciplinary action needed.

But as I mention for minor issues like I mentioned earlier, you can give them a verbal warning first and monitor them to see if there is any improvement, if not you can then give them a written warning, most stores nowadays have these written warning forms where you fill in the action that they took which was not proper or the job that did not perform even after a prior verbal warning.

Once you give them a copy of that, ask them to sign it and keep a copy of it in their employment file. I usually terminate an employee if he or she makes the same violation within 30 days of giving them the written warning.

9. SETTING UP TARGET & GOAL ORIENTED INCENTIVES

I do this often in my stores. I set up certain goals and offer incentives if they reach the goal. You can be very creative when comes to creating an incentive program, but it depends on what type of restaurant you have. I have done the same with Deli food, where I set up a daily target and a weekly target and if they reached that goal each employee got an incentive pay.

10. REGULAR EMPLOYEE MEETINGS AND COACHING

Last but not the least, it is very important to have regularly scheduled employee meetings and coaching, meet every month, where you tell them of any upcoming changes in your store, and them ask for any issues they faced that month or any concern they have and this is the time also to roll out any new incentives plan you have for them for the following month. Offer them tips words of encouragement and remind them to greet and make eye contact with each customer, also emphasize the cleaning regiment and keeping their assigned tables clean.

MENU DEVELOPMENT

PRICING

Start menu planning and development early in the game, the same time you develop your theme and concept.

A major way of ensuring profit is your menu. You must balance food cost, the price charged, and a balance between inexpensive items and expensive items.

Food cost is about 30%-35%. So, for every $1.00 you pay for a food item, you need to charge a minimum of $3.34.

Food cost is the menu price. Cost of food is how much you paid for the ingredients.

Food costs are made up of ingredients and everything else in your restaurant from payroll to rent, or mortgage payment. The food is bought and paid for, someone must prepare it, it must be cooked, served and cleaned up afterwards.

Go back to your high school algebra. The formula is:

Cost of your product /.35

Look at a New York Strip dinner:

Steak = $4.50/portion, your cost

Wrap = $2.50/plate (Potato, veg, salad, bread, and condiments)

Steak=$5.00/portion

Wrap=$2.50

$7.50/.35 = $21.43

$21.43 is the absolute minimum. However, it is an awkward number. You could put $21.50 or $21.99 on your menu. This brings your food cost just at 30%, bring in more profit.

Menu items and prices must be appropriate to the kind of dining place you are operating, your overhead, as well as competition. But, don't undersell yourself.

Balance your menu with expensive and less expensive items. Perhaps a fabulous burger with lettuce, tomato, onion, and fries. The cost to you $3.00. Your cost-plus profit is now $8.57. Offer other up-sell options and favorite choices, maybe even a signature burger. With various cheese, mushrooms, avocado, etc. the cost goes up to $3.30. Your food cost is now $9.43.

While you are pricing your cost of food, you must further determine if a specific item belongs on your menu.

For instance, your overhead cost, cost of food, and drink plus tax comes to $15.00 for a lunch dish. Let's say that your customer only wants to pay $10.00-$11.00 for that same lunch. This lunch item should come off your menu.

On the other hand, some items on your menu are loss leaders. Much like a retail store. Something is sold at cost or slightly above because your specific target market will add appetizers, drinks, and dessert.

This brings up portion control. You are giving away your profits if you put too much food on a plate. Conversely, you are losing customers if there is less food than expected. Customers then feel this is a great deal or a bad value respectively.

Your business will reflect the results immediately. You will either be eating into your profits or losing customers.

Chain restaurants and franchises have this down to a science. Every dish must be the exact same every time. Same weight, same look. Practicing portion control begins with measuring every item.

Meat and seafood must be measured. Cheese and some other condiments can be stored already in portion control packages. Others can be measured with a measuring cup. Vegetables and mashed potatoes, for instance.

Eventually, you can eyeball portions. However, double-check your 'eyeball' amount every so often. It has a way of getting away from you.

Let's say you're offering a certain weight of steak, say 4-oz. It must be exactly 4 oz. And, the baked potato must be the exact weight you have determined, every single time.

You could offer an option between a 4-oz. and a 6-oz. steak. Or, you can offer a ¼ lb. or ½ pound hamburger. Or split the burgers down into a plate of sliders. Steaks, fish, shrimp, chicken breast can be purchased already packaged in portion control packages.

The same goes for sandwiches and salads. For sandwiches count out number of meat and cheese slices, possibly a different price point for certain variations of bread. Add in condiments and each topping such as lettuce and tomato, etc.

Keep track of your wholesale price of food items. Seasonal changes, weather and gas prices can change at any time. Adjust cost of food, i.e., menu prices, accordingly.

The way to do this goes back to balancing your menu between expensive and less expensive items. Expensive items are more susceptible to price variables while less expensive items are more likely to remain steady.

Determining what dishes and items you will serve, at what cost, what balance. Not just balance between expensive versus inexpensive but also proteins, any specials, gluten-free, organic, etc.

Don't get into the time and expense of changing your menu every few weeks. If you use a chalkboard, white board or your own printed-out menu cards changes are easier to make.

You may be using these types of menus for a fast casual or fast food restaurant. Additionally, you could take advantage of a menu posted with changing letters and numbers.

Casual restaurants and up don't typically use these fast-change types of menus. Therefore, the importance of balance between expensive and less expensive menu items.

Expensive lobster might be listed at "Market Price, " and expensive beef stays at a 35% profit price. Offset these dishes with lower-priced pasta in various formats sauces and toppings, and/or various chicken dishes.

Understand your cost of food, price fluctuation, portion control, maintaining a balanced menu and customer expectations. These are changes you can count on when crunching numbers and determining profits and revenue.

Before moving on to the creative aspect of designing your menu, let's outline a few additional things to study, research and be aware of that concern your menu.

Some restaurant owners price their items on a gross margin basis. Determine what you should make per item and add that to your cost of food.

According to Cornell University and the National Restaurant Associate 60% of restaurants fail within the first three years of opening, and after five the number may climb as high as 75%.

The best restaurant chains average a net profit at or over 30% of sales. With consistent returns like this, you could pay your investment off in at least three years. An awesome ROI.

Restaurants can fail because they don't have a unique selling point. Why should your customers come to your restaurant versus your competitors'? And, surprise, great food, and service are not a unique selling point. Everyone is advertising the same thing.

It goes back to your concept, theme, passion, and emotion. The WHY you are in the food industry business.

Having too large a menu is a major downfall. Remember, you can't be everything to everybody? If you try, you won't be anything let alone anything special.

Your large menu is confusing to customers and lacks focus.

Large menus require more ordering time, slower table service, a larger inventory of food, longer ticket times, equipment and cooks. The longer this takes, the less amount of time you are making profits.

Can you negotiate prices? You need to know what other restaurants are paying for food items and make your suppliers compete for your business. You know the saying, 'there's a sucker in every negotiation.' Don't let it be you.

CREATIVE PRODUCTION

Your menu development and design are not random decisions. They are a significant part of your restaurant concept. Your menu defines you.

Menus will vary by the concept. Some will be busy with a lot of information crammed into every nook and cranny. Some will be big and plastic coated. Maybe on a chalk or whiteboard.

Franchises and chains do not allow room for any changes or creativity in your menu. It comes ready, set and to go. Independently owned restaurants no matter the size or type of restaurant develop their own look and type of menu.

Regardless of style or format, you use to distribute your menus there are tried and true guidelines. Some of these you may never have thought about. However, menus have everything to do with the impact you make on your customers, carrying out your theme and giving focus to your food.

A cost-effective, profitable menu is of small or moderate size, as in a number of dishes offered. The main message is the dishes you're known for, the food that separates you from the rest and can be supplemented by seasonal and short-term offers.

You have your theme and concept in place, you know your target market and the food you are going to serve so now it is time to make everything work together. What holds it together is the core menu.

The core menu is your product line. It's American, Japanese, Pizza, Italian, Mexican, Fine Dining, Sandwiches, etc. The rest is secondary. For instance, appetizers desserts and beverages.

- Your menu needs professional help. You may have brought your chef in early in the game or from the beginning of your build out. (S)he plays a significant role in the development of your menu as in the pricing, but also in the layout.

- Keep descriptions of food simple and easy to understand. A couple of options under each category with wait staff trained to answer any questions a customer may have.

- Your menu should stand-out and offer things the customer can't find anywhere else.

- Print more than you think you will need.

You can use your own word processor to layout items by category. If your menu is being printed professionally, a rough layout is what you will need to give to a printer or professional.

If you have a lot of talent and want to take on the job yourself check out software programs such as Canva. There is a free version as well as a professional version you can use.
Canva is in photo-shop style and results in professional looking work. Write your text in one of their layout formats and upload pictures. Basically, you are developing your restaurant's template.

Canva offers an enormous amount of creativity, stock covers and menus and a lot of guidance and help.

Lightspeed is another source for designing your menu. They guide you through the process including where to put pricing and the use of dollar signs.

However you implement your menu, it speaks volumes about you, your restaurant and food. Be creative and check into menu trends every so often to keep an updated, fresh look.

Right now, a big trend is Plant-Based food and menus. OK, so this is a term that lets you take liberties with the traditional vegan/vegetarian menu items. You include lesser amounts of meat, dairy and other types of protein.

A Plant-Based menu is heavy on the more health conscience fruits, vegetables, and vegetarian trends. For instance, mashed cauliflower kale, pizza with healthy crusts, and vegetable-based risottos.

Street food is poised for to go upscale and mainstream. Not just for trucks anymore, street food is going the catered route as well becoming specialties in restaurants as globally inspired menu items.

Forbes predicts a growing trend of exotic options beyond chicken and beef. Examples are venison, bison, and elk. While not a brand-new trend it is expanding along with artisan butchery and butcher to table choices.

The National Restaurant Association has been discussing sustainable seafood for the last several years. This includes environmentally friendly farm-raised seafood such as tuna, salmon but also blue and blackfish.

Other trends are Mediterranean flavors, nose-to-tail, and root-to-leaf. Be on a constant look-out for food industry news and customer-demanded trends. The smart thing to do would be adjusting them if you can do whatever style restaurant you have.

Trends may not take over your entire menu. Maybe they are specials and maybe you slowly add them if they are appropriate to your restaurant style. The reason for careful consideration of trend foods is, one, you never want to follow what you think will only be a passing trend and, two, your menu items are where you maximize your profits.

Food that maximizes your profit is number one. Therefore, you should:

Layout your menu to promote and show off the most-profitable menu items. These are low-cost ingredients you can sell at high-market prices.

Use some design tricks on your menu that emphasize what you want your customers to order. Graphically feature profitable items.

Relative pricing is a trick you have fallen for even if you didn't know it. This is when a restaurant using relative pricing to make other items more attractive. For instance, a dish priced at $32.00 makes the $20.00 item look attractive.

This tactic is often used in wine sales. It's called the decoy method. Your pricing columns show an expensive bottle or glass of wine near a less expensive, higher-profit choice.

Best and most profitable menu items go at the top of their category.

Include pictures in your menu of featured dishes.

Your menu should have one section of only specials. Some diners will order these discounted menu choices, others will order what they want anyway. The specials are a hook. Remember the kids' options.

POS ACCOUNTING AND BOOKKEEPING

A Point of Sale (POS) system is a computer system linking together all areas of the restaurant. It provides smooth workflow, provides the bookkeeping function and tracks inventory. It can be calibrated to track inventory specific to your restaurant.

You need it, it is a big deal, and it will save money. Some restaurant owners choose to install a POS after operating a week or so to determine their specific needs. Some restaurants won't use one at all, or a variation fit for the size and type of restaurant.

POS provides vital data and increases profits:

- The system reports your best and worst-selling menu items or services you provide. Therefore, you can even make changes on the fly.
- You can run promotions, and specials and your POS gives you data reporting on what worked, what didn't and any benefits.
- You can plan on the fly or in real time. You will know your busiest days. Your POS system tracks them and reports to you the bestsellers, on which days. You then have vital information on what to stock, order and what products are hurting your bottom line.
- Your POS monitors salaries, number of hours worked, tracks employee sales and progress, as well as tips earned.

A POS system costs between a low-end of $2,000 up to over $15,000. You then have a monthly fee and a processing fee for credit and debit cards.

As a computerized process, the POS system can be expanded with the growth of your business. Growth can be defined by the increase of sales in your existing location or the addition of locations.

According to a survey implemented by Top Restaurant POS Systems, the most recommended POS restaurant systems are:

REVEL SYSTEMS

9.8 Outstanding

- Retail
- Quick Service
- Restaurants
- Medium/Large Businesses
- 1+ Year Manufacturer's Warranty
- Completely Customizable

TOUCHBISTRO RESTAURANT

9.4

- Restaurants
- Quick Service
- For Restaurants of ANY Size
- "Best Restaurant POS" of 2015 and 2016
- Boosts Sales and Bottom Lines

HARBORTOUCH

8.4

- Retail
- Quick Service
- Restaurants
- 24/7 Customer Service
- Lifetime Equipment Warranty
- 30-Day Risk-Free Trial

TOAST

8.1

- Restaurants

- Quick Service
- Free 24/7 Support
- Custom-Built for Restaurants
- Real-Time Analytics and Updates

LIGHTSPEED

7.8

- Retail
- Restaurants
- Quick Service
- Medium/Large Businesses
- 30-Day Lightspeed Warranty
- Retail Focused Solution

POS Systems are also available by specific restaurant types. For instance, pizza, diners, and food trucks. White table-cloth fine dining, whatever type of establishment you have chosen.

Your POS system allows for your remote management of the restaurant and come tax season you can say goodbye to the mountain of paperwork and receipts.

MARKETING DEVELOPMENT

THE REAL GAME

Yelp

Social Media

These are the two must haves, don't even think of not using them, 82% of business from millennials comes through social media. This is where the action is, and the game is played.

1. Get your free page on Yelp as soon as possible. Log on to their website, sign up and add photos, add a Yelp Deal.

   Yelp provides the ability to add deals, photos, messaging and viewing businesses.

   You will be up and running in a matter of minutes. According to Yelp, listings with photos keep visitors on that page 2½ times longer than others.

2. Yelp and Bing are joining forces. Yelp information is now integrated into Bing Local Pages. Searchers are now able to scan your restaurant, location, and reviews directly from their Bing results.

3. Yelp releases mobile data often. Previously they reported:

   - *Yelpers called a local business **every other second** via the mobile application.*
   - ***35 percent of all searches** on Yelp.com came from a Yelp mobile app.*
   - ***Every other second** a consumer had generated directions to a local business.*
   - *A photo was uploaded **every 30 seconds** from a Yelp mobile app.*

   You can purchase reports from Yelp at around $3.00 to keep up with trends and identify innovative ideas for your restaurant.

4. Build an app right away.

5. Michael Lukianoff, Fishbowl's Chief Analytics Officer, told CNBC in an interview that "social media gives smaller, independent, and regional [brands] a level playing ground to get their message/voice out."

   The industry is telling you that you are not competing successfully with other restaurants if you are not on social media. As the competition heats up, the stronger your presence on social media should be.

   The key social media formats are Facebook, Twitter, Pinterest, LinkedIn, and Google+.

6. Start your own blog, be sure to tweet often, use Instagram and Facebook. Get a good camera, or use a professional, and take tempting photos of your food. Post them. Pictures of your food are de rigueur for social media.

7. Blogging has been known to increase lead generation by 89%. Nurture these potential, loyal customers.

8. Build ordering or reservation making on your Facebook page. An 'Order Now' call to action.

9. Offer coupons on Facebook and other social media. Include specials and holiday events, TGIFs, graduations, whatever fits in with your style.

10. Always respond to comments and complaints made by followers. Good or bad. Positively resolve issues in the public forum. Use the opportunities to thank customers, offer rewards, etc.

11. Find food bloggers and make them your friends. It's unbelievable how much promotion gets done through blogs. Even niche-marketing.

Invite your food bloggers to share recipes, even host an event just for them. Business is built on teamwork, making bonds with people involve others.

12.   Get on YouTube. Show off your restaurant, have your chef or employees demonstrate a recipe. Show your location.

13.   Build a professional, functional and attractive but fun website.

14.   Capture information from each website visitor building a target market list.

15.   Capture customer phone numbers from call-ins give discounts, vouchers, and coupons to customers who volunteer their information.

16.   With data that can be used for target marketing, use e-mail autoresponder technology to send gifts and awards for occasions, etc.

17.   A very cool idea being used by many businesses, services and with restaurants catching on is building a Keeping in Touch with Your Tribe for your website landing page.

Your website landing page should load in a matter of a couple seconds. It's noted that the human attention span is about eight seconds.

You can test that on yourself. How quickly do you move off a website if you don't see what you are looking for immediately?

Attention span gets shorter as the customer moves to mobile devices. So, set your tone and message to get immediate attention. Don't use a bunch of fancy or complex code. Just develop as a WordPress blog on the website for starters.

Your landing page has one purpose. That is to communicate to your visitor, repeat customer, food bloggers, in other words, your tribe. What does the landing page do? Keeps you and your customers in touch, and provides them with interesting information.

For instance, you are advertising a new seasonal menu, giving first access to special occasion menus, a new recipe or food rewards club. The message you put on your landing page should be clear and relevant.

The landing page should be about that one thing and nothing else. Use it as an opportunity to talk about something new, get your visitors' feedback, opinions, and personal data.

TRADITIONAL MARKETING AND PR

In addition to Yelp, social media and your website landing page you can choose various traditional advertising and marketing formats.

Traditional advertising and marketing include radio, TV, print, billboards. The signage outside or on your building, painted on the windows. Your logo as a Chamber of Commerce and Better Business Bureau member.

Except for PR, traditional print, TV, radio, billboard, signage is expensive. Stretch your advertising dollars over the opportunities that provide a good ROI.

Take, for example, a press release for your new chef. Invite a local food editor to your restaurant. For smaller and fast food restaurants, take out ads with offers in local papers, shoppers and neighborhood magazines.

Smaller budgets and smaller restaurants can sponsor local sports teams. Little League, high school, whatever you can manage in your budget. Provide jerseys, if possible.

Donate food or sponsor catering for community events or disasters. Partner up with a delivery service. Work to extend and deepen that relationship. Get some PR out of it.

The most important rules of your core marketing program are:

- Your target market must know you exist. This means being unique. This applies to the quality of food, service, friendliness, and cleanliness. Don't be unforgettable.

- You must get your customers talking about you. Of course, the best advertising is word of mouth. Every customer that visits your restaurant should feel as though they have had a real treat. If they don't have a pleasant experience, they won't be back. And, anything they have to say will not be good.

- Messages you put out into the public must be clear, concise and direct. Everyone gets hit with thousands of marketing and advertising messages every day.

Many consumers are so desensitized to these messages and just tune them out. Therefore, you need something quick and clear. For example, "Got Milk?", "Have it Your Way."

- You and your restaurant must be involved in the community. Be the single sponsor of a good community cause. Don't just show up or put your restaurant's name on a T-Shirt, get involved. People remember those that commit to helping them.

- Marketing starts before you even open your restaurant. If you are not an expert, hire one. At least short term. You need to take advantage of all PR and marketing opportunities. It will be worth every single dime you spend for a professional who knows the restaurant industry.

There are dozens of ways to promote your restaurant. Identify those that make you stand out. Spend money on the big ROI opportunities. And, work hard behind the scenes for the opportunities that are free, or almost.

THE OPENINGS

SOFT OPENING

A soft opening is done before you open to the public. It's nonofficial and usually, involves a private party. Friends, family, club members, media types, sports groups, etc. This is a private party of whoever you want to invite so you can test the systems, give the employees practice and host the party free of charge.

Afterwards, ask your guests how it went, did they like the food, how was the service, can they help you with any comments and advice? You could possibly use anonymous comment cards.

Afterwards, meet with your employees and discuss the pros and cons of the event. Together analyze what needs attention, take in recommendations and the guest's comment cards. When things are adjusted, then silently open your doors.

Reread the section on Pop-Ups as a viable alternative to soft openings or pre-openings.

PRE-OPENING

This is the silent opening after the soft opening. When all issues have been addressed, operate for a few more weeks. Silently opened to the public. Maybe some social media and flyers. But, no big grand opening yet.

This gives you and your staff additional experience and opportunities to identify what is working and what is not. It could be food, pricing, service, something with the facility, payment or POS kinks, delivery issues. This is a double check for you before the big day.

GRAND OPENING

When you and the staff have built-up confidence and all systems are good to go, you are ready for the grand opening you have been waiting for from the start of this dream.

This is the time to break out your organized, detailed plan. Prepare a written plan, a timeline but don't jump the gun until you are confident and have backup plans for any bombshells that may happen.

Do not ignore mobile marketing!

In life, there is never a second chance to make a first great impression. Your grand opening is exactly that, the first chance to make a great impression. This is the event you have been waiting for to present your brand. Do it up right.

First, invite the media. As discussed, any restaurant critics, publishers of the small papers, community shopper papers, magazines and community target marketing materials.

Invite some VIPs. A Mayor, councilman, influencers and taste makers. Seat these two groups close together and have the head chef or you, the owner, visit the tables.

Invite your banker!

Make sure all names of guests are noted with the hostess. They should be recognized, not kept waiting and given impeccable service. You could possibly have entertainment or a short speech made by a community leader or the manager of the center where you are renting your space.

Hold an old-fashioned ribbon cutting for the first opening days' lunch.

Have grand opening specials. Date night, Mom and Dad's night out, mommy's luncheon. Have buy-one-get-one-free (BOGO) offers. Don't give out unrelated gifts or the impression you will or will not buy anything from the guests.

Have a special event for the businesses around you or just their owners. Have an administrative assistant's lunch, or week, offer to hold public and special private events such as fundraisers.

Give out food samples to passers-by. Or, have radio remote broadcasts if they are popular in your area and supply food from your restaurant, or cater events at a discounted price.

Have press-kits and introduction materials ready to distribute. Have more than you think you will need on hand. Include copies of your menu, your cover story, your plans, introduction to you and your staff. Everything a media person needs and everything a market influencer wants.

SUMMARY OF KEYS TO SUCCESS

You have now read about the parts and pieces that go into opening a restaurant. Things such as:

- Great concept, theme, idea
- Stick to your concept
- Don't try to be all things to all people
- Implement research
- Write a knock-out business plan
- Overestimate capital needs
- Importance of your Menu
- Plus, plus, plus, plus

Becoming a successful restaurant owner is not just challenging. The margins are small, labor and food costs are high, and it takes years of dedication and demanding work to build a reputation. What more can you do?

BE EXTRAORDINARY, BE REMARKABLE

Average food, average service, and forgettable experiences will not draw people into your restaurant.

You must stand out. You have to magically turn your restaurant into the place that people will talk about and recommend to everyone they meet.

Have a unique, or better than the rest, concept, stay true to your brand and allow it to show in every aspect of your restaurant. The décor, menu, food offerings, lighting, entrance. Everything you do makes up your brand. Everything.

HAVE A SIMPLE BUT DELICIOUS MENU

A huge menu with multiple-on-top-of-multiple selections is a great theory. But not great in reality.

Twelve or so choices are enough. Most people don't need anything other than some meat, chicken, fish, and vegetables. Maybe some pasta, but no one needs eight styles of chicken at a steakhouse. Or ten types of wings anywhere, unless you're Hooters.

You want to be known for your signature dishes, or sandwiches, or appetizers. You want to be known for something, and something good. Serve fresh and amazing ingredients in each dish.

Some styles of restaurants may need a lot of items on their menu. For instance, a casual seafood restaurant on the waterfront. But, maybe several of the dishes could be replaced with a fewer higher quality menu items.

Find a way where twenty-three menu items don't just sit in the kitchen, burning in the warming pot, hoping someone will order them before you must throw everything away. And, don't resort to frozen seafood that is advertised as 'fresh' on your menu.

WELL THOUGHT-OUT SEATING

Moving people through your restaurant is what makes profits. Right? To serve as many as possible, and still make your customers feel comfortable.

A successful restaurant must serve as many diners as possible with a smart yet expansive layout.

SIGNAGE

The presentation is everything. Most diners from off the street will pick a place to eat by what they see. The sign, the number of cars in the parking lot, etc.

An old, unlit sign, or poorly lit and in bad condition sign is not the impression you want to give to potential diners. People certainly won't think the food is any better inside than the sign is outside.

A NO-FRILLS, APPROPRIATE ATMOSPHERE

People may not care whether some restaurants have paper napkins or high-end cotton or if there's a tablecloth. People want what is appropriate to your style, theme and the food you serve.

Tables, chairs and interesting things on the walls. It all varies by type of restaurant, from fast food to fine dining. People expect ambiance and decoration appropriate to your theme and in good taste.

PERSONABLE WAIT STAFF

No matter what, your wait staff and customer service people must be memorable. In an effective way. Fun to be around. Appropriate to your style of restaurant.

People go out for the experience, and for entertainment. No matter the price range, the food, and the experience will keep them coming back. Plus, they will recommend you to their friends.

LOCATION, PARKING, AND CONVENIENCE

In the city, you need foot traffic. You want to be easy to see and convenient for your customers. In the suburbs, you need plenty of parking, lighting and handicap parking and ramps.

MEMORABILIA

Think of the Hard Rock brand. Every location has a store for customers to buy souvenirs. Anything from leather jackets to keychains. Many American and all European locations still have packs of matches with their name and location advertised.

Of course, memorabilia are not possible for every type of restaurant, or even necessary. But for some, leave a little something around. For instance, if you are a casual restaurant and do catering or take away, have printed menus for diners to take with them.

If you're a deli or sandwich shop, have takeaway menus. All bags, boxes and take away containers should have your name printed on them.

If you're a famous Chinese restaurant, have wait staff wear black T-shirts with white Peking Duck letters across the front or some very cool logo. People may be interested in buying something like that. Or a seafood bar/restaurant with monogrammed glasses or mugs.

If you do a pop-up restaurant get the name, opening date, something, even just a menu that people won't be able to leave behind. A T-shirt, anything cute. No trashy shot glasses, stickers or out-of-date T-shirts. Unique and cool, or not at all. But, don't miss any chances to get free advertising.

SOCIAL MEDIA

Do it or die! No longer the future of marketing, it is the marketing. Get on Twitter, Facebook, and Instagram. Be sure to get on Yelp, post specials on Foursquare.

Post photos, invite diners to post photos on your blog, along with fun content. Allow reservations and take away orders to be placed via social media and a mobile app.

Do what it takes. Whatever it takes. Grow your online presence. Get and keep a loyal social media community.

PAY ATTENTION TO THE SMALL STUFF

A diner in your restaurant should never have to ask for more napkins, more water, utensils or a 'clean' anything.

When a customer has to track down a wait person they get annoyed. What if they haven't seen their person in a while and must ask someone else to find them? Or trip them as they go by to get their attention? These are not good things.

People don't like paying for that kind of service, and they won't be back for more of it, either.
You should go through the entire dining process yourself and identify the speed bumps.

After that, fix them. Have friends come in every so often and get their feedback. Use the mystery shopper or mystery diner concept.

GET FREE PRESS AND PR

- Guest chefs, contests, tasting parties. Any clever ideas you can come up with to get free press coverage. Some others:
- Loyalty program.
- Selectively call local media and invite them for a free meal in return for coverage or a mention in a local magazine or food section of the paper.
- Your name and website should come up first in online restaurant searches and directories.
- You and your staff should be involved in your community and local events.
- Advertise your sensitivity to diet restrictions and demands.
- Be in your Chamber of Commerce and registered with the Better Business Bureau.
- Advertise on Bing Pages.
- Keep your Name, Address and Phone (NAP) numbers in the same order, and the same everywhere they appear. Consistency equals weight from Google.

- Advertise on Facebook.
- On your web page respond to all comments.
- While setting up your social media don't forget to add a mobile app.

'WHAT'S HOT' CULINARY FORECAST

The National Restaurant Association's annual What's Hot culinary forecast predicts food and menu trends for the coming year. For 2017, the NRA surveyed nearly 1,300 professional chefs to find out what the hottest menu trends were.

Number One

"Menu trends today are beginning to shift from ingredient-based items to concept-based ideas, mirroring how consumers tend to adapt their activities to their overall lifestyle philosophies, such as environmental sustainability and nutrition. Also among the top trends for 2017, we're seeing several examples of house-made food items and various global flavors, indicating that chefs and restaurateurs are further experimenting with from-scratch preparation and a broad base of flavors."

- Hudson Riehle, senior vice president of the National Restaurant Association's research and knowledge group.

IS IT YOUR TIME?

HERE ARE A FEW STATISTICS FROM THE NATIONAL RESTAURANT ASSOCIATION THAT TELL THE STORY.

Food and drink sales of the restaurant industry in the United States is over 746 billion U.S. dollars and growing.

More than 195 million U.S. consumers visited a sit-down restaurant in the spring of 2016.

During the same time, over 216 million Americans visited a fast-food place.

68% of Americans try new restaurants based on recommendations by friends.

46% of smartphone users use their phones at least once a month to order takeout or delivery.

70% of adults say that the availability of healthy menu options would make them choose one restaurant over another.

In conclusion, the industry is exploding, there are multitudes of fresh, new and exciting ideas and opportunities available. It's a great time in the industry and in the United States to start living your dream right now.

LAST WORDS

I want to say THANK YOU for purchasing and reading this book. I really hope you got a lot out of it!

Can I ask you for a quick favor though?

If you enjoyed this book, I would really appreciate it if you could leave me a Review on Amazon.

I LOVE getting feedback from my wonderful readers, and reviews on Amazon really do make the difference. I read all of my reviews and would love to hear your thoughts.

Thank you so much!!

APPENDIX A

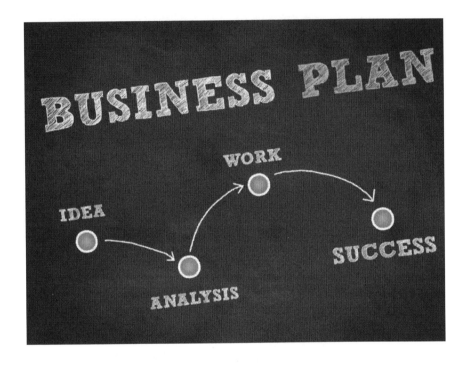

1.0 EXECUTIVE SUMMARY

On the Water is a new Mediterranean restaurant on the Sunset Strip. On the Water will target both fun-seeking as well as sophisticated diners looking for good food in a fascinating atmosphere. On the Water will seek to earn 85% gross margins through an innovative setting, a wonderful menu, and an experienced restaurateur.

The Market

On the Water will be targeting locals and tourists who are active restaurant seekers. There will be a special focus on young adults with $15K-$60K of income looking for good food and a great time. In addition to the young adults with money to spend, On the Water will also be targeting adults and tourists known to frequent Sunset Blvd. The general demographics are males and females ages 20-50 with some or all of a college education. In addition to local Hollywood area people, On the Water will also serve party animals from neighboring cities and tourists.

Historically, if there is a dip in the general economy, the restaurant industry is usually effected far less that the overall economy. To some degree this is because of people's perception that food, regardless whether it is from the grocery or a restaurant is a fundamental necessity of life and spend accordingly.

The Service and Products

One thing that is always consistent with On the Water is their impeccable service. All server staff hired have extensive experience and all go through three weeks of training, ensuring benchmarked customer service. On the Water's services are all delivered in their extraordinary atmosphere which includes a comprehensive art and culture collection from Mediterranean Europe. This provides an authentic surrounding that at times seems to distract everyone as they analyze the wealth of artifacts on display.

The menu is Lily Valdivia's pride. It is a culmination of over 20 years of cooking. The menu contains traditional favorites such as hummus, baba ganouj, and tabouli. These favorites are differentiated through the use of the freshest organic ingredients. Most people are not aware of how much better the items taste when they are prepared with the freshest ingredients and made with love. Other menu items are kebobs, chutneys, flat breads and desserts. Everything is fresh, homemade, and prepared daily.

Management

The restaurant is led by Lily Valdivia, an industry veteran. Her restaurant experience began 12 years ago as a server. She quickly moved up to fine dining serving where she perfected her formal, customer-centric serving approach. For the last five years Lily has been the manager at a European restaurant with over $2.5 million in annual sales. As mentioned earlier, Lily started cooking 20 years ago as a child in Greece. Lily came from a large family and it quickly became her responsibility to cook for the entire family. Her mother, who had three generations of traditional recipes, trained her. Lily quickly mastered these and began experimenting with her own dishes. The feedback from her family was always very positive. She knew one day she would have to parlay this skill into a business opportunity.

On the Water is forecasted to reach profitability by month two. Sales are forecasted to reach $1,785,000 by year two and grow to $2,345,000 by year three. We forecast a high net profit on these sales.

1.1 OBJECTIVES

1. Sales increasing to more than $2,345,000 by the third year.
2. Keeping gross margin at approximately 80%.

3. Improve inventory turnover to two-hundred turns next year in year two, and to 240 in year three.

1.2 MISSION

On The Water is a business that envelopes fine dining of unique Mediterranean taste and an excellent bar and grill atmosphere. The mission is not only to have great tasting food, but have efficient and friendly service. Our dining environment is not only welcoming and sophisticated, it is unique in design, with walls on almost all sides that are constantly wet with running water and a lush jungle ceiling that will hang from above. We concentrate on customer satisfaction and quality food that is always fresh and specially selected. We will not judge a customer on class or dress. We want the On The Water grill to be place people can enjoy a good meal and meet new friends at our tropical

Mediterranean Honey bar located inside the restaurant.

CHART: HIGHLIGHTS

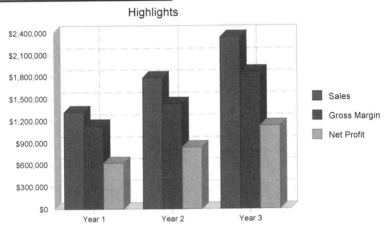

2.0 COMPANY SUMMARY

On The Water creates and serves a wild atmosphere for dining and eloquent Mediterranean feasts for people who love the restaurant and bar scene, as well as a good time spent out on the town. Its customers are creative, fun-seeking, and sophisticated diners who wish to be best served by the restaurant they choose.

2.1 COMPANY OWNERSHIP

On The Water is a sole-proprietorship business owned in majority by its founder and president Lily Valdivia. The business employs the owner, one investor and eight employees.

2.2 START-UP SUMMARY

Our start-up expenses come to $61,450 which is mostly expensed equipment, rent, and legal and consulting costs associated with opening our first restaurant. We also require $69,000 of start-up assets, which includes $22,000 cash and $45,000 of long-term assets. The start-up costs are to be financed some by direct owner investment, as well as with the help of a major investor.

CHART: START-UP

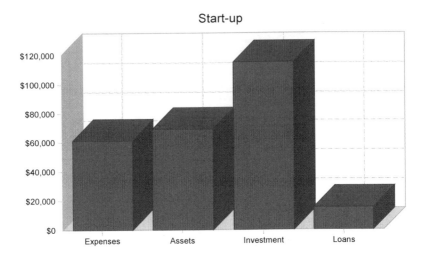

TABLE: START-UP

Start-up	
Requirements	
Start-up Expenses	
Legal	$500
Stationery etc.	$750
Menus	$200
Consultants	$1,000
Insurance	$1,000
Rent	$6,000
Expensed equipment	$50,000
Other	$2,000
Total Start-up Expenses	$61,450
Start-up Assets	
Cash Required	$22,000
Start-up Inventory	$2,000
Other Current Assets	$0
Long-term Assets	$45,000
Total Assets	$69,000
Total Requirements	$130,450

Table: Start-up Funding

Start-up Funding	
Start-up Expenses to Fund	$61,450
Start-up Assets to Fund	$69,000
Total Funding Required	$130,450
Assets	
Non-cash Assets from Start-up	$47,000
Cash Requirements from Start-up	$22,000
Additional Cash Raised	$0
Cash Balance on Starting Date	$22,000
Total Assets	$69,000
Liabilities and Capital	
Liabilities	
Current Borrowing	$0
Long-term Liabilities	$0
Accounts Payable (Outstanding Bills)	$15,450
Other Current Liabilities (interest-free)	$0
Total Liabilities	$15,450
Capital	
Planned Investment	
Investor 1	$85,000
Other	$30,000
Additional Investment Requirement	$0
Total Planned Investment	$115,000
Loss at Start-up (Start-up Expenses)	($61,450)
Total Capital	$53,550
Total Capital and Liabilities	$69,000
Total Funding	$130,450

3.0 PRODUCTS AND SERVICES

On The Water provides delicious mediterranean cuisine, with friendly, efficient service and atmosphere. We are especially focused on providing a unique environment for people to dine and meet. We have a full Mediterranean Honey bar for young adults and adults to enjoy drinks and music. We also provide the value of flawless and creative staff at a "hip" location located on Sunset Strip with valet included.

4.0 MARKET ANALYSIS SUMMARY

On The Water focuses on local and tourist active restaurant seekers, with special focus on young adults with a $20-30,000/year income and a desire for good food and a fascinating atmosphere as our target market.

4.1 MARKET SEGMENTATION

Our target market segmentation is divided between young restaurant seekers with money to spend, as well as other adults and tourists who are known to frequent Sunset Blvd. for recreational enjoyment. Defining the high-end crowd is difficult because most of Sunset Strip goers are such.

We generally know the characteristics of our clientele with our available demographics of the area, our personal crowd would consist of young adults (ages 20-29) and adults (ages 30-50), both male and female, usually at least one year of college if not already fully graduated. Our geographics include people from the local Hollywood area, party animals from other neighboring cities, and tourists from other states and countries. The psychographics of our clientele include "yuppies, big spenders, club hoppers, baby boomers, Sunset rats, etc..." The buying patterns of our clientele will be people who like to spend money on pampering themselves, on quality food, feeling special, projecting an image of wealth, trying new things, and thrill seeking.

CHART: MARKET ANALYSIS (PIE)

Market Analysis (Pie)

- Young adults
- Adults

TABLE: MARKET ANALYSIS

Market Analysis		Year 1	Year 2	Year 3	Year 4	Year 5	
Potential Customers	Growth						CAGR
Young adults	8%	638,949	686,870	738,385	793,764	853,296	7.50%
Adults	5%	1,152,870	1,210,514	1,271,040	1,334,592	1,401,322	5.00%

Total	5.91%	1,791,81 9	1,897,38 4	2,009,42 5	2,128,35 6	2,254,61 8	5.91 %

4.2 TARGET MARKET SEGMENT STRATEGY

On The Water will focus on attracting young adults and adults ages 20-55, with an annual income of at least $15,000 to $60,000. We will concentrate on the high-end spenders who enjoy new restaurants, eating out, a fun atmosphere, and high-end food and service. We want the yuppies, baby boomers, high-end clubbers, tourists with money, wealthy image seekers and compulsive spenders. We focus on these specific groups because these are the types of people who frequent other clubs and restaurants like ours on Sunset Blvd. They are the ones that are willing to spend their money on good dining and service at high prices.

We generally know the characteristics of our clientele with our available demographics of the area, our personal crowd would consist of young adults and adults ages 20-55, both male and female, usually at least one year of college if not already fully graduated. Our geographics include people from the local Hollywood area, party animals from other neighboring cities, and tourists from other states and countries. The psychographics of our clientele include "yuppies, big spenders, club hoppers, baby boomers, Sunset rats, etc..." The buying patterns of our clientele will be people who like to spend money on pampering themselves, on quality food, feeling special, projecting an image of wealth, trying new things, and thrill seeking.

5.0 STRATEGY AND IMPLEMENTATION SUMMARY

The following sections outline the strategy and implementation summary for On The Water.

5.1 SALES STRATEGY

The important elements of the sales forecast are shown in the following table. The sales of food, drinks, and merchandise take a while to grow but will near $2 million in the second year.

TABLE: SALES FORECAST

Sales Forecast			
	Year 1	Year 2	Year 3
Unit Sales			
Covercharge	0	0	0
Meals	38,277	57,000	63,000
Drinks	147,136	180,000	196,000
Restaurant Merchandise	1,225	3,000	3,500
Total Unit Sales	186,638	240,000	262,500
Unit Prices	Year 1	Year 2	Year 3
Covercharge	$0.00	$0.00	$0.00
Meals	$15.00	$15.00	$18.00
Drinks	$5.00	$5.00	$6.00
Restaurant Merchandise	$8.00	$10.00	$10.00
Sales			
Covercharge	$0	$0	$0
Meals	$574,155	$855,000	$1,134,000
Drinks	$735,680	$900,000	$1,176,000
Restaurant Merchandise	$9,800	$30,000	$35,000
Total Sales	$1,319,635	$1,785,000	$2,345,000
Direct Unit Costs	Year 1	Year 2	Year 3
Covercharge	$0.00	$0.00	$0.00
Meals	$3.00	$4.00	$5.00
Drinks	$0.50	$0.60	$0.75
Restaurant Merchandise	$3.00	$4.00	$4.50
Direct Cost of Sales			
Covercharge	$0	$0	$0
Meals	$114,831	$228,000	$315,000
Drinks	$73,568	$108,000	$147,000
Restaurant Merchandise	$3,675	$12,000	$15,750
Subtotal Direct Cost of Sales	$192,074	$348,000	$477,750

CHART: SALES MONTHLY

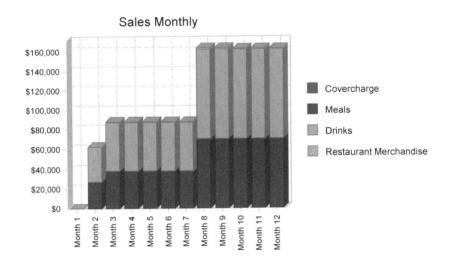

Sales Monthly

CHART: SALES BY YEAR

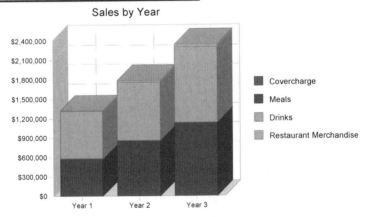

Sales by Year

5.2 MILESTONES

The following table lists important program milestones, with dates and managers in charge, and budgets for each. The milestone schedule indicates our emphasis on planning for implementation. The most important programs are the sales and marketing programs listed in detail in the previous topics.

TABLE: MILESTONES

Milestones					
Milestone	Start Date	End Date	Budget	Manager	Department
Getting all furniture for restaurant	11/4/2000	11/13/2000	$3,000	LVM	Design
Getting jungle decorations for ceiling	11/4/2000	11/18/2000	$600	LVM	Design
Valet preparations	10/5/2000	10/14/2000	$500	LVM	Management
Painting/reconstuction of restaurant	9/4/2000	10/16/2000	$2,000	LVM	Design
Buying food for opening	10/28/2000	10/29/2000	$500	LVM	Food
Creation and distribution of fliers	11/4/2000	1/20/2001	$1,000	LVM	Promotional
Website	9/1/2000	10/1/2000	$1,000	LVM	Management
Production and completion of menus	10/1/2000	10/30/2000	$400	LVM	Design
Buying all	8/1/2000	10/4/2000	$7,000	LVM	Management

supplies for kitchen					
Staff Schedules	8/1/2000	8/15/2000	$0	LVM	Management
Totals			$16,000		

CHART: MILESTONES

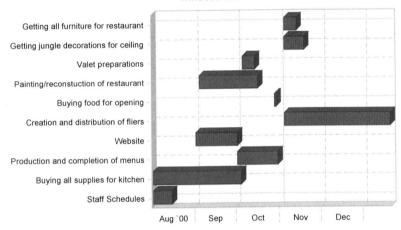

Milestones

6.0 MANAGEMENT SUMMARY

Our management philosophy is based on responsibility and mutual respect. People who work at On The Water want to work there because we have an environment that encourages creativity and achievement. The team includes a maximum of eight to twelve employees, under a president/manager of one.

6.1 PERSONNEL PLAN

The personnel plan reflects what we would like to keep as a steady positioning throughout the years. Our total headcount will increase from 8 to 12 come June because that's the beginning of our "good" season. However, we plan to keep the head count at 12 because of the space and dynamics of the restaurant. It appears we don't need more than 12 employees to run the business untill the fourth and fifth year, if and when we are successful enough to expand. Detailed monthly projections are included in the appendix.

TABLE: PERSONNEL

Personnel Plan	Year 1	Year 2	Year 3
Management	$41,580	$45,738	$50,312
Hostess	$16,170	$17,787	$19,566
Waiters/Waitresses	$55,860	$61,446	$67,591
Bartenders	$27,540	$30,294	$33,323
Bus Boys	$7,920	$8,712	$9,583
Cocktail Waitresses	$3,360	$3,696	$4,066
Chefs	$73,920	$81,312	$89,443
Total People	12	12	12
Total Payroll	$226,350	$248,985	$273,884

7.0 FINANCIAL PLAN

The following topics and tables outline our financial plan. We plan to turn a significant profit, but we will structure the business so as to maintain a healthy cash flow.

7.1 IMPORTANT ASSUMPTIONS

The financial plan depends upon important assumptions, most of which are shown in the following table. The key underlying assumptions are:

- We assume a slow-growth economy, without major recession.
- We assume that there are no unforseen changes in the expectancy in the popularity of our restaurant.
- We assume access to investments and financing are sufficient to maintain and fulfill our financial plan as shown in the tables.

TABLE: GENERAL ASSUMPTIONS

General Assumptions			
	Year 1	Year 2	Year 3
Plan Month	1	2	3
Current Interest Rate	10.00%	10.00%	10.00%
Long-term Interest Rate	10.00%	10.00%	10.00%
Tax Rate	25.42%	25.00%	25.42%
Other	0	0	0

7.2 BREAK-EVEN ANALYSIS

For our Break-even Analysis, we assume running costs which include our full payroll, rent, and utilities, and an estimation of other running costs.

CHART: BREAK-EVEN ANALYSIS

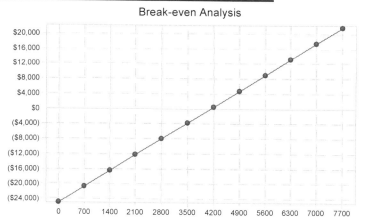

Break-even Analysis

TABLE: BREAK-EVEN ANALYSIS

Break-even Analysis	
Monthly Units Break-even	4,117
Monthly Revenue Break-even	$29,113
Assumptions:	
Average Per-Unit Revenue	$7.07
Average Per-Unit Variable Cost	$1.03
Estimated Monthly Fixed Cost	$24,875

7.3 PROJECTED PROFIT AND LOSS

The most important assumption in the Projected Profit and Loss statement is the gross margin. Although it doesn't jump drastically in the first year, over given time the restaurant will develop its customer base and name, and the growth will pick up more rapidly towards the fourth and fifth years of business. The increase in gross margin will be due to a slow increase in sales prices and an increase in customer base, which is critical. Month-by-month assumptions for profit and loss are included in the appendix.

CHART: GROSS MARGIN MONTHLY

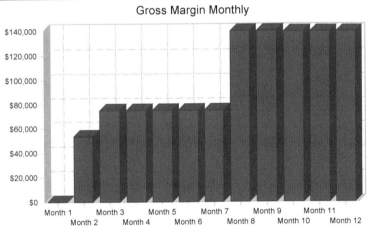

Gross Margin Monthly

CHART: GROSS MARGIN YEARLY

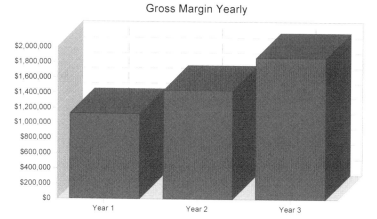

Gross Margin Yearly

TABLE: PROFIT AND LOSS

Pro Forma Profit and Loss	Year 1	Year 2	Year 3
Sales	$1,319,635	$1,785,000	$2,345,000
Direct Cost of Sales	$192,074	$348,000	$477,750
Other	$0	$0	$0
Total Cost of Sales	$192,074	$348,000	$477,750
Gross Margin	$1,127,561	$1,437,000	$1,867,250
Gross Margin %	85.44%	80.50%	79.63%
Expenses			
Payroll	$226,350	$248,985	$273,884
Sales and Marketing and Other Expenses	$2,200	$200	$300
Depreciation	$0	$0	$0
Insurance	$0	$0	$0
Rent	$36,000	$36,000	$36,000
Utilities	$0	$0	$0
Leased Equipment	$0	$0	$0
Payroll Taxes	$33,953	$37,348	$41,083
Other	$0	$0	$0
Total Operating Expenses	$298,503	$322,533	$351,266
Profit Before Interest and Taxes	$829,059	$1,114,467	$1,515,984
EBITDA	$829,059	$1,114,467	$1,515,984
Interest Expense	$0	$0	$0
Taxes Incurred	$207,115	$278,617	$385,313
Net Profit	$621,944	$835,850	$1,130,671
Net Profit/Sales	47.13%	46.83%	48.22%

CHART: PROFIT MONTHLY

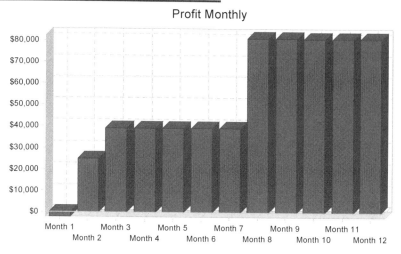

Profit Monthly

CHART: PROFIT YEARLY

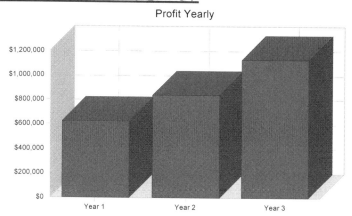

Profit Yearly

7.4 PROJECTED CASH FLOW

The cash flow depends on assumptions for inventory turnover, payment days, and accounts receivable management. Our projected same-day collection is critical, and also reasonable and expected in the restaurant industry. We don't expect to need that much continued support even when we reach the less profitable months, as they are expected.

TABLE: CASH FLOW

Pro Forma Cash Flow	Year 1	Year 2	Year 3
Cash Received			
Cash from Operations			
Cash Sales	$1,319,635	$1,785,000	$2,345,000
Subtotal Cash from Operations	$1,319,635	$1,785,000	$2,345,000
Additional Cash Received			
Sales Tax, VAT, HST/GST Received	$0	$0	$0
New Current Borrowing	$0	$0	$0
New Other Liabilities (interest-free)	$0	$0	$0
New Long-term Liabilities	$0	$0	$0
Sales of Other Current Assets	$0	$0	$0
Sales of Long-term Assets	$0	$0	$0

	Year 1	Year 2	Year 3
New Investment Received	$0	$0	$0
Subtotal Cash Received	$1,319,635	$1,785,000	$2,345,000
Expenditures	Year 1	Year 2	Year 3
Expenditures from Operations			
Cash Spending	$226,350	$248,985	$273,884
Bill Payments	$455,248	$727,844	$925,510
Subtotal Spent on Operations	$681,598	$976,829	$1,199,394
Additional Cash Spent			
Sales Tax, VAT, HST/GST Paid Out	$0	$0	$0
Principal Repayment of Current Borrowing	$0	$0	$0
Other Liabilities Principal Repayment	$0	$0	$0
Long-term Liabilities Principal Repayment	$0	$0	$0
Purchase Other Current Assets	$0	$0	$0
Purchase Long-term Assets	$0	$0	$0
Dividends	$0	$0	$0
Subtotal Cash Spent	$681,598	$976,829	$1,199,394
Net Cash Flow	$638,037	$808,171	$1,145,606
Cash Balance	$660,037	$1,468,208	$2,613,814

CHART: CASH

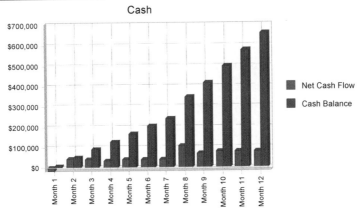

7.4 PROJECTED BALANCE SHEET

The projected Balance Sheet is quite solid. We do not project any real trouble meeting our debt obligations, as long as we can achieve our specific goals.

TABLE: BALANCE SHEET

Pro Forma Balance Sheet	Year 1	Year 2	Year 3
Assets			
Current Assets			
Cash	$660,037	$1,468,208	$2,613,814
Inventory	$25,988	$58,344	$60,691
Other Current Assets	$0	$0	$0
Total Current Assets	$686,025	$1,526,551	$2,674,506
Long-term Assets			
Long-term Assets	$45,000	$45,000	$45,000
Accumulated Depreciation	$0	$0	$0
Total Long-term Assets	$45,000	$45,000	$45,000
Total Assets	$731,025	$1,571,551	$2,719,506
Liabilities and Capital	Year 1	Year 2	Year 3
Current Liabilities			
Accounts Payable	$55,531	$60,207	$77,490
Current Borrowing	$0	$0	$0
Other Current Liabilities	$0	$0	$0
Subtotal Current Liabilities	$55,531	$60,207	$77,490
Long-term Liabilities	$0	$0	$0
Total Liabilities	$55,531	$60,207	$77,490
Paid-in Capital	$115,000	$115,000	$115,000

Retained Earnings	($61,450)	$560,494	$1,396,344
Earnings	$621,944	$835,850	$1,130,671
Total Capital	$675,494	$1,511,344	$2,642,016
Total Liabilities and Capital	$731,025	$1,571,551	$2,719,506
Net Worth	$675,494	$1,511,344	$2,642,016

7.6 BUSINESS RATIOS

Business ratios for the years of this plan are shown below. Industry profile ratios based on the Standard Industrial Classification (SIC) code 5812, Eating places, are shown for comparison.

TABLE: RATIOS

Ratio Analysis	Year 1	Year 2	Year 3	Industry Profile
Sales Growth	n.a.	35.26%	31.37%	7.60%
Percent of Total Assets				
Inventory	3.56%	3.71%	2.23%	3.60%
Other Current Assets	0.00%	0.00%	0.00%	35.60%
Total Current Assets	93.84%	97.14%	98.35%	43.70%
Long-term Assets	6.16%	2.86%	1.65%	56.30%
Total Assets	100.00%	100.00%	100.00%	100.00%
Current Liabilities	7.60%	3.83%	2.85%	32.70%
Long-term Liabilities	0.00%	0.00%	0.00%	28.50%
Total Liabilities	7.60%	3.83%	2.85%	61.20%
Net Worth	92.40%	96.17%	97.15%	38.80%
Percent of Sales				
Sales	100.00%	100.00%	100.00%	100.00%

Gross Margin	85.44%	80.50%	79.63%	60.50%
Selling, General & Administrative Expenses	38.33%	65.53%	56.44%	39.80%
Advertising Expenses	0.00%	0.00%	0.00%	3.20%
Profit Before Interest and Taxes	62.82%	62.44%	64.65%	0.70%
Main Ratios				
Current	12.35	25.35	34.51	0.98
Quick	11.89	24.39	33.73	0.65
Total Debt to Total Assets	7.60%	3.83%	2.85%	61.20%
Pre-tax Return on Net Worth	122.73%	73.74%	57.38%	1.70%
Pre-tax Return on Assets	113.41%	70.92%	55.74%	4.30%
Additional Ratios	Year 1	Year 2	Year 3	
Net Profit Margin	47.13%	46.83%	48.22%	n.a
Return on Equity	92.07%	55.31%	42.80%	n.a
Activity Ratios				
Inventory Turnover	10.81	8.25	8.03	n.a
Accounts Payable Turnover	8.92	12.17	12.17	n.a
Payment Days	28	29	27	n.a
Total Asset Turnover	1.81	1.14	0.86	n.a
Debt Ratios				
Debt to Net Worth	0.08	0.04	0.03	n.a
Current Liab. to Liab.	1.00	1.00	1.00	n.a
Liquidity Ratios				
Net Working Capital	$630,494	$1,466,344	$2,597,016	n.a
Interest Coverage	0.00	0.00	0.00	n.a
Additional Ratios				
Assets to Sales	0.55	0.88	1.16	n.a
Current Debt/Total Assets	8%	4%	3%	n.a
Acid Test	11.89	24.39	33.73	n.a
Sales/Net Worth	1.95	1.18	0.89	n.a
Dividend Payout	0.00	0.00	0.00	n.a

TABLE: PERSONNEL

Personnel Plan		Month 1	Month 2	Month 3	Month 4	Month 5	Month 6	Month 7	Month 8	Month 9	Month 10	Month 11	Month 12
Management	0%	$0	$3,780	$3,780	$3,780	$3,780	$3,780	$3,780	$3,780	$3,780	$3,780	$3,780	$3,780
Hostess	0%	$0	$1,470	$1,470	$1,470	$1,470	$1,470	$1,470	$1,470	$1,470	$1,470	$1,470	$1,470
Waiters/Waitresses	0%	$0	$4,410	$4,410	$4,410	$4,410	$4,410	$4,410	$5,880	$5,880	$5,880	$5,880	$5,880
Bartenders	0%	$0	$0	$2,430	$2,430	$2,430	$2,430	$2,430	$3,078	$3,078	$3,078	$3,078	$3,078
Bus Boys	0%	$0	$720	$720	$720	$720	$720	$720	$720	$720	$720	$720	$720
Cocktail Waitresses	0%	$0	$0	$0	$0	$0	$0	$0	$672	$672	$672	$672	$672
Chefs	0%	$0	$4,620	$4,620	$4,620	$4,620	$4,620	$4,620	$9,240	$9,240	$9,240	$9,240	$9,240
Total People		0	8	8	8	8	8	8	12	12	12	12	12
Total Payroll		$0	$15,000	$17,430	$17,430	$17,430	$17,430	$17,430	$24,840	$24,840	$24,840	$24,840	$24,840

TABLE: GENERAL ASSUMPTIONS

General Assumptions	Month 1	Month 2	Month 3	Month 4	Month 5	Month 6	Month 7	Month 8	Month 9	Month 10	Month 11	Month 12
Plan Month	1	2	3	4	5	6	7	8	9	10	11	12
Current Interest Rate	10.00%	10.00%	10.00%	10.00%	10.00%	10.00%	10.00%	10.00%	10.00%	10.00%	10.00%	10.00%
Long-term Interest Rate	10.00%	10.00%	10.00%	10.00%	10.00%	10.00%	10.00%	10.00%	10.00%	10.00%	10.00%	10.00%
Tax Rate	30.00%	25.00%	25.00%	25.00%	25.00%	25.00%	25.00%	25.00%	25.00%	25.00%	25.00%	25.00%
Other	0	0	0	0	0	0	0	0	0	0	0	0

TABLE: CASH FLOW

Pro Forma Cash Flow		Month 1	Month 2	Month 3	Month 4	Month 5	Month 6	Month 7	Month 8	Month 9	Month 10	Month 11	Month 12
Cash Received													
Cash from Operations													
Cash Sales		$0	$62,560	$88,125	$88,125	$88,125	$88,125	$88,125	$163,770	$163,770	$162,970	$162,970	$162,970
Subtotal Cash from Operations		$0	$62,560	$88,125	$88,125	$88,125	$88,125	$88,125	$163,770	$163,770	$162,970	$162,970	$162,970
Additional Cash Received													
Sales Tax, VAT, HST/GST Received	0.00%	$0	$0	$0	$0	$0	$0	$0	$0	$0	$0	$0	$0
New Current Borrowing		$0	$0	$0	$0	$0	$0	$0	$0	$0	$0	$0	$0
New Other Liabilities (interest-free)		$0	$0	$0	$0	$0	$0	$0	$0	$0	$0	$0	$0
New Long-		$0	$0	$0	$0	$0	$0	$0	$0	$0	$0	$0	$0

	Month 1	Month 2	Month 3	Month 4	Month 5	Month 6	Month 7	Month 8	Month 9	Month 10	Month 11	Month 12
term Liabilities												
Sales of Other Current Assets	$0	$0	$0	$0	$0	$0	$0	$0	$0	$0	$0	$0
Sales of Long-term Assets	$0	$0	$0	$0	$0	$0	$0	$0	$0	$0	$0	$0
New Investment Received	$0	$0	$0	$0	$0	$0	$0	$0	$0	$0	$0	$0
Subtotal Cash Received	$0	$62,560	$88,125	$88,125	$88,125	$88,125	$88,125	$163,770	$163,770	$162,970	$162,970	$162,970

Expenditures	Month 1	Month 2	Month 3	Month 4	Month 5	Month 6	Month 7	Month 8	Month 9	Month 10	Month 11	Month 12
Expenditures from Operations												
Cash Spending	$0	$15,000	$17,430	$17,430	$17,430	$17,430	$17,430	$24,840	$24,840	$24,840	$24,840	$24,840
Bill Payments	$15,520	$3,054	$30,881	$35,738	$31,680	$31,680	$31,680	$32,959	$69,637	$57,846	$57,127	$57,446
Subtotal Spent on Operations	$15,520	$18,054	$48,311	$53,168	$49,110	$49,110	$49,110	$57,799	$94,477	$82,686	$81,967	$82,286
Additional Cash Spent												
Sales Tax, VAT, HST/GST	$0	$0	$0	$0	$0	$0	$0	$0	$0	$0	$0	$0

Paid Out Principal Repayment of Current Borrowing	$0	$0	$0	$0	$0	$0	$0	$0	$0	$0	$0	$0
Other Liabilities Principal Repayment	$0	$0	$0	$0	$0	$0	$0	$0	$0	$0	$0	$0
Long-term Liabilities Principal Repayment	$0	$0	$0	$0	$0	$0	$0	$0	$0	$0	$0	$0
Purchase Other Current Assets	$0	$0	$0	$0	$0	$0	$0	$0	$0	$0	$0	$0
Purchase Long-term Assets	$0	$0	$0	$0	$0	$0	$0	$0	$0	$0	$0	$0
Dividends	$0	$0	$0	$0	$0	$0	$0	$0	$0	$0	$0	$0
Subtotal Cash Spent	$15,520	$18,054	$48,311	$53,168	$49,110	$49,110	$49,110	$57,799	$94,477	$82,686	$81,967	$82,286
Net Cash Flow	($15,520)	$44,506	$39,814	$34,957	$39,015	$39,015	$39,015	$105,971	$69,293	$80,284	$81,003	$80,684
Cash Balance	**$6,480**	**$50,986**	**$90,800**	**$125,757**	**$164,772**	**$203,787**	**$242,802**	**$348,773**	**$418,066**	**$498,350**	**$579,353**	**$660,037**

TABLE: BALANCE SHEET

Pro Forma Balance Sheet		Month 1	Month 2	Month 3	Month 4	Month 5	Month 6	Month 7	Month 8	Month 9	Month 10	Month 11	Month 12
Assets	Starting Balances												
Current Assets													
Cash	$22,000	$6,480	$50,986	$90,800	$125,757	$164,772	$203,787	$242,802	$348,773	$418,066	$498,350	$579,353	$660,037
Inventory	$2,000	$2,000	$9,948	$14,147	$14,147	$14,147	$14,147	$14,147	$26,318	$26,318	$25,988	$25,988	$25,988
Other Current Assets	$0	$0	$0	$0	$0	$0	$0	$0	$0	$0	$0	$0	$0
Total Current Assets	$24,000	$8,480	$60,935	$104,947	$139,904	$178,919	$217,934	$256,949	$375,091	$444,384	$524,338	$605,341	$686,025
Long-term Assets													
Long-term Assets	$45,000	$45,000	$45,000	$45,000	$45,000	$45,000	$45,000	$45,000	$45,000	$45,000	$45,000	$45,000	$45,000
Accumulated Depreciatio	$0	$0	$0	$0	$0	$0	$0	$0	$0	$0	$0	$0	$0

n													
Total Long-term Assets	$45,000	$45,000	$45,000	$45,000	$45,000	$45,000	$45,000	$45,000	$45,000	$45,000	$45,000	$45,000	$45,000
Total Assets	$69,000	$53,480	$105,935	$149,947	$184,904	$223,919	$262,934	$301,949	$420,091	$489,384	$569,338	$650,341	$731,025
Liabilities and Capital	Month 1	Month 2	Month 3	Month 4	Month 5	Month 6	Month 7	Month 8	Month 9	Month 10	Month 11	Month 12	
Current Liabilities													
Accounts Payable	$15,450	$2,030	$29,685	$34,682	$30,624	$30,624	$30,624	$30,624	$67,708	$55,942	$55,212	$55,531	$55,531
Current Borrowing	$0	$0	$0	$0	$0	$0	$0	$0	$0	$0	$0	$0	$0
Other Current Liabilities	$0	$0	$0	$0	$0	$0	$0	$0	$0	$0	$0	$0	$0
Subtotal Current Liabilities	$15,450	$2,030	$29,685	$34,682	$30,624	$30,624	$30,624	$30,624	$67,708	$55,942	$55,212	$55,531	$55,531
Long-term Liabilities	$0	$0	$0	$0	$0	$0	$0	$0	$0	$0	$0	$0	$0
Total Liabilities	$15,450	$2,030	$29,685	$34,682	$30,624	$30,624	$30,624	$30,624	$67,708	$55,942	$55,212	$55,531	$55,531
Paid-in Capital	$115,000	$115,000	$115,000	$115,000	$115,000	$115,000	$115,000	$115,000	$115,000	$115,000	$115,000	$115,000	$115,000
Retained Earnings	($61,450)	($61,450)	($61,450)	($61,450)	($61,450)	($61,450)	($61,450)	($61,450)	($61,450)	($61,450)	($61,450)	($61,450)	($61,450)

Earnings	$0	($2,100)	$22,700	$61,715	$100,730	$139,745	$178,760	$217,775	$298,832	$379,896	$460,576	$541,260	$621,944
Total Capital	$53,550	$51,450	$76,250	$115,265	$154,280	$193,295	$232,310	$271,325	$352,383	$433,442	$514,126	$594,810	$675,494
Total Liabilities and Capital	$69,000	$53,480	$105,935	$149,947	$184,904	$223,919	$262,934	$301,949	$420,091	$489,384	$569,338	$650,341	$731,025
Net Worth	$53,550	$51,450	$76,249	$115,265	$154,280	$193,295	$232,310	$271,325	$352,383	$433,442	$514,126	$594,810	$675,494

APPENDIX –B

PERSONAL FINANCIAL STATEMENT

Personal Financial Statement of:

John Doe

1/1/2017

Assets	Amount in Dollars
Cash - checking accounts(2)	12,450.29
Cash - savings accounts(1)	46,231.10
Certificates of deposit	15,000.00
Securities - stocks / bonds / mutual funds	76,891.45
Notes & contracts receivable	17,321.63
Life insurance (cash surrender value)	28,531.00
Personal property (autos, jewelry, etc.)	197,451.88
Retirement Funds (eg. IRAs, 401k)	32,100.00
Real estate (market value)	312,000.00

Inventory Cash Value	28,700.00
Other assets (specify)	0.00
Total Assets	**766,677.35**

Liabilities	**Amount in Dollars**
Current Debt (Credit cards, Accounts)	14,765.14
Notes payable (Auto)	7,979.65
Taxes payable	4,155.12
Real estate mortgages (describe)	177,881.45
Other liabilities (HELOC)	0.00
Other liabilities (specify)	0.00
Total Liabilities	**204,781.36**
Net Worth	**561,895.99**

Signature:...................... **Date:**

Made in the USA
Monee, IL
20 January 2020